HOUSING FOR THE ELDERLY IN 2010

Projections and Policy Options

URBAN INSTITUTE REPORT 89–4

Harold M. Katsura,
Raymond J. Struyk, and
Sandra J. Newman

THE URBAN INSTITUTE PRESS
Washington, D.C.
July 1989

THE URBAN INSTITUTE PRESS
2100 M Street, N.W.
Washington, D.C. 20037

Library of Congress Cataloging in Publication Data

Housing for the Elderly in 2010: Projections and Policy Options

1. Aged--Housing--United States. 2. Aged--Housing--Government policy--United States. I. Struyk, Raymond J. II. Newman, Sandra J. III. Title. IV. Series.

HD7287.92.U54K37 1989 363.5′946′.973 89-9141

(Urban Institute Reports; 89-4, ISSN 0897-7399)

ISBN 0-87766-474-9
ISBN 0-87766-473-0 (casebound)

Printed in the United States of America.

9 8 7 6 5 4 3 2 1

Distributed by University Press of America

4720 Boston Way
Lanham, MD 20706

3 Henrietta Street
London WC2E 8LU ENGLAND

URBAN INSTITUTE REPORTS are designed to provide rapid dissemination of research and policy findings. Each report contains timely information and is rigorously reviewed to uphold the highest standards of policy research and analysis.

The Urban Institute is a nonprofit policy research and educational organization established in Washington, D.C., in 1968. Its staff investigates the social and economic problems confronting the nation and government policies and programs designed to alleviate such problems. The Institute disseminates significant findings of its research through the publications program of its Press. The Institute has two goals for work in each of its research areas: to help shape thinking about societal problems and efforts to solve them, and to improve government decisions and performance by providing better information and analytic tools.

Through work that ranges from broad conceptual studies to administrative and technical assistance, Institute researchers contribute to the stock of knowledge available to public officials and private individuals and groups concerned with formulating and implementing more efficient and effective government policy.

Conclusions or opinions expressed in Institute publications are those of the authors and do not necessarily reflect the views of other staff members, officers or trustees of the Institute, advisory groups, or any organizations that provide financial support to the Institute.

CONTENTS

Abstract
Executive Summary

1 Policy Context, Methodology, and Data 1
Policy Context 2
Methodology and Data 6
Microsimulation with the Transfer Income Model 7
Additional Housing Data 8
Key Assumptions 12
Caveats in Interpreting the Results 13

2 Projected Changes in the Characteristics and Housing Situation of the Elderly Population if Current Policies Continue 15
Projected Changes in the Characteristics of U.S. Households 15
Housing Needs of the Elderly in 2010 Under the Base Case 18
General Housing Attributes 19
Activity Limitations and Dwelling Modifications 24
Deficiencies and Housing Finance 28
Alternative Projections 34
Alternative Assumptions about Living Arrangements 35
Alternative Assumptions about Housing Preferences 35
Sensitivity of the Projections to the Changed Assumptions 37

3 Impacts of an Expanded Housing Allowance Program for Renters 49
Simulating a Voucher Program 51
Determining Household Eligibility 51

Calculating Voucher Payments 51
Participation in a Voucher Program 52
Simulation Results 53
Program Costs and Participation 55
Impact of Housing Conditions 56

4 Housing Allowances for Homeowners 63
Simulating a Homeowner Voucher Program 64
Simulation Results 65
Participation and Costs 66
Impact on Housing Conditions 68

5 The Effects of an Increase in the use of Home Equity Conversion Mortgages 75
Home Equity Conversion Mortgages 75
Fixed Debt Loans without Guaranteed Lifetime Tenure 75
Fixed Debt Loans with Guaranteed Lifetime Tenure 76
Rising Debt Loans for Tax Deferral 76
Combination Loan-Equity Plans 77
Simulating an Increase in the Use of HECM 78
Simulation Results 80
Characteristics of the Eligible Population 80
Impact on Housing Conditions 82

6 The Impacts of a Congregate Housing Voucher Program 87
Simulating a Congregate Housing Voucher Program 89
Simulation Results 90
Characteristics of Eligible Households 91
Impact on Housing Conditions 93

7 Summary and Comparison of the Initiatives 99
Impacts on the Housing of Eligible Households 100
Expanded Housing Vouchers for Renters 101
Housing Vouchers for Homeowners 101
Expanded Use of Home Equity Conversion Mortgages 104

Congregate Housing Vouchers 106
Costs, Political Feasibility, and Impacts on the Housing of Participants 106

Appendices

A Adding AHS Variables to the Aged CPS Files 113
B Additional Adjustments Considered for the Main Simulations, and Additional Tables 121
C Population and Household Projections to 2010 Used in TRIM2 127
D Economic Projections and Transfer Program Assumptions Used in TRIM2 Projections to 2010 157
E Adding 1983 AHS Variables to the 1978 AHS File 171

Tables

1.1 Average Annual Growth in Selected Economic Factors: 1985-2010 8

1.2 Housing Variables Added to the CPS File 9

1.3 Predictive Equations Estimated for Adding AHS Variables to the CPS 10

2.1 Distribution of Households by Household Type and Age of Head: 1985 and 2010 16

2.2 Distribution of Households by Households Type for Selected Age Groups: 1985-2010 17

2.3 Changes in Mean Real Household Income by Type of Household: 1984-2010 17

2.4A General Housing Attributes by Tenure in 1978 and 2010 20

2.4B General Housing Attributes by Age in 1978 and 2010 21

2.4C General Housing Attributes by Household Type in 1978 and 2010 22

2.4D General Housing Attributes by Income Quartile in 1978 and 2010 23

2.5A Activity Limitations and Dwelling Modifications by Tenure: 1978 and 2010 25

2.5B Activity Limitations and Dwelling Modifications by Age of Household Head: 1978 and 2010 25

2.5C Activity Limitations and Dwelling Modifications by Household Type: 1978 and 2010 27

2.6A Deficiencies and Housing Finances by Tenure: 1978 and 2010 31

2.6B Deficiencies and Housing Finance by Age of Household Head in 1978 and 2010 31

2.6C Deficiencies and Housing Finances by Household Type in 1978 and 2010 32

2.6D Deficiencies and Housing Finances by Income Quartiles in 1978 and 2010 33

2.7 Distribution of the Elderly among Living Arrangements in 2010, Base Case and Alternative 36

2.8 Selected Housing Attributes by Tenure in 2010 under Different Assumptions 38

2.9 Selected Housing Attributes by Age of Head in 2010 under Different Assumptions 39

2.10 Selected Housing Attributes by Household Type in 2010 under Different Assumptions 40

2.11 Selected Housing Attributes by Income Quartile in 2010 under Different Assumptions 42

3.1 Percentage of Eligible Renter Households Becoming Housing Allowance Recipients in the Supply Experiment under the 50% of Area Median Income Eligibility Rule 53

3.2 Selected Housing Attributes of All Elderly Renters and Eligible Renters in 2010 54

3.3 Participation and Costs under Three Alternative Voucher Programs in 2010 56

3.4 Selected Housing Attributes of Eligible Renters before and after Implementation of an Expanded Voucher Program in 2010 57

3.5 Selected Housing Attributes of Eligible Renters before and after Program Implementation, by Income Quartile 58

3.6 Selected Housing Attributes of Eligible Renters before and after Program Implementation, by Age 58

3.7 Selected Housing Attributes of Eligible Renters before and after Program Implementation, by Household Composition 59

4.1 Selected Housing Attributes of All Elderly Homeowners and Eligible Homeowners in 2010 66

4.2 Participation and Costs under Three Alternative Homeowner Voucher Programs in 2010 68

4.3 Selected Housing Attributes of Eligible Homeowners before and after Implementation of a Voucher Program in 2010 70

4.4	Selected Housing Attributes of Eligible Homeowners before and after Program Implementation, by Income Quartile	70
4.5	Selected Housing Attributes of Eligible Homeowners before and after Program Implementation, by Household Composition	71
5.1	Examples of Monthly Payments under the Century Plan	79
5.2	Selected Housing Attributes of All Elderly Homeowners and Eligible Homeowners in 2010	81
5.3	Selected Housing Attributes of Eligible Homeowners before and after an Increase in the Use of HECMs in 2010	82
5.4	Selected Housing Attributes of Eligible Homeowners before and after an Increase in the Use of HECMs in 2010, by Income Quartile	83
5.5	Selected Housing Attributes of Eligible Homeowners before and after an Increase in the Use of HECMs in 2010, by Household Type	84
6.1	Participation and Annual Costs under a Congregate Housing Program in 2010	91
6.2	Selected Housing Attributes of All Elderly Households and Households Eligible for a Congregate Housing Program in 2010	92
6.3	Selected Housing Attributes of Eligible Households before and after Implementation of a Congregate Housing Program in 2010	94
6.4	Selected Housing Attributes of Eligible Households before and after Implementation of a Congregate Housing Program, by Household Composition	95

6.5	Selected Housing Attributes of Eligible Households before and after Implementation of a Congregate Housing Program, by Income Quartile	97
7.1	Impacts on Housing of Participants and Costs of Different Policy Options in 2010	108
A.1	Summary of Parameter Estimates for Equations Used to Add Housing Variables to the CPS	112
A.2	Variable Definitions	118
B.1	Selected Attributes of Elderly-Headed Households by Tenure in 1978	124
B.2	Deficiencies which Cause a Housing Unit to be Judged Physically Inadequate - Based upon AHS Items, Revised Definition (1981)	125
C.1	Population Projections to 2010	129
C.2A	Unpublished Census Household Projections -- Series B; Husband-Wife Households by Age of Head and Year	136
C.2B	Unpublished Census Household Projections -- Series B; Female Family Heads by Age of Head and Year	137
C.2C	Unpublished Census Household Projections -- Series B; Male Family Heads by Age of Head and Year	138
C.2D	Unpublished Census Household Projections -- Series B; Female Primary Individuals by Age of Head and Year	139
C.2E	Unpublished Census Household Projections -- Series B; Male Primary Individuals by Age of Head and Year	140
C.2F	Unpublished Census Household Projections -- Series B; Projected Number of Total Households by Age of Head and Year	141

C.3 Census Household Projections by Age of Head and Household Type: 2000 144

C.4A U.S. Household Projections to 2010 Based on Census Series B; by Household Type and Age of Head Class 146

C.4B Number of Households in the Base Year (1984) by Household Type and Age of Head Class 147

C.4C IWM: Initial Weight Multipliers by Household Type and Age of Head Class 147

C.5 Scaling Factors by Household Type and Number of Adults Class 150

C.6A Simulation Year Households by Household Type by Age of Head Class 151

C.6B Simulation Year Persons by Sex by Race by Age Class 152

C.7 Simulated Households Compared to Projected Households 153

C.8 Simulated Population Compared to Project Population 154

D.1 TRIM2 Income Variables Aggregate and Detailed Sources 158

D.2 TRENDLONG Economic Projections from DRI 160

D.3 Weighted Aggregate Personal Income 162

D.4 Income by Source After Economic Aging to 2010 164

D.5 Adjustments to SSI Participation 167

D.6 Assumptions Used in Simulating SSI to 2010 167

E.1 Summary of Parameter Estimates for Equations Used to Add 1983 AHS Variables to the 1978 AHS 174

E.2 Variable Definitions 176

E.3 Deficiencies which Cause a Housing Unit to be Judged Physically Inadequate - Based upon AHS Items, Revised Definition (1981) 177

E.4 Regional Change in Housing Values: 1978-1984 179

Figures

1.1 Growth and Aging of U.S. Population: 1985-2010 3

7.1 Impact of Expanded Housing Program for Renters on Housing Problems of Eligibles 102

7.2 Impact of Housing Voucher Programs for Homeowners on Problems of Eligibles 103

7.3 Impact of Increase Use of HECMs on Housing Problems of Eligible Households 105

7.4 Impact of Congregate Housing Voucher Program on Housing Problems of Eligibles 107

ABSTRACT

This study uses microsimulation to project the characteristics of the elderly in the year 2010, and their housing needs. It then it projects the impacts on those needs of continuing current housing policies versus four policy alternatives--expanded housing vouchers for low-income elderly renters, housing vouchers for low-income elderly homeowners, expanded availability of Home Equity Conversion Mortgages (HECMs), and congregate housing vouchers for low-income impaired elderly.

Making housing vouchers for low-income elderly an entitlement would add $3.3 billion dollars a year to the housing assistance budget and help 1.5 million participants. Making housing vouchers for low-income homeowners an entitlement would add $5.2 billion a year and help 2.76 million participants. Both would help housing quality. Expanded HECMs would help about 670,000 participants but would do little for housing quality because little would be spent on upgrading. A congregate housing voucher program would add $1.2 billion annually to the budget, and would help 650,000 participants. Its benefits would be greater than these numbers suggest, because they would go to the elderly who most need housing assistance if they are to avoid institutionalization.

EXECUTIVE SUMMARY

The aging of the population, combined with the need to control the federal budget deficit, places a high premium on meeting the needs of the elderly in the most efficient way. One of these needs is housing. Little information has been available so far on which to base housing policy decisions for the future. This report starts to fill the gap by projecting the effects of different housing policy alternatives on the housing needs of the elderly in the areas of excess cost burden, structural deficiencies, and mainte-nance deficiencies.

METHODOLOGY AND DATA

The analysis is based on The Urban Institute's micro-simulation Transfer Income Model (TRIM2). TRIM is the latest in a family of static models and is used primarily in the area of government tax and transfer programs. For this analysis TRIM2 was run on the March Current Population Survey (CPS) for 1984, augmented with information from the 1978 Annual Housing Survey (AHS) and the 1981 Survey of Residential Finance. In addition to strictly housing attributes, some variables regarding the presence of activity limitations of the household head or spouse were included.

The model ages the CPS data file by adjusting the sample weights to reflect growth and change in the population, by adjusting labor force variables to reflect changes in employment and dollar amounts to reflect inflation and real economic growth. Census projections of the number of households by age of head of household and household type for the year 2010 were used as the population targets in the TRIM2 aging procedure.

The report contains projections about the effects of continuing current policies through 2010 under four sets of assumptions which differ in the way they project living arrangements and housing preferences. For most housing variables the projections are similar. Size of unit and home equity holdings, however, are quite sensitive to assumptions. Alternative policies are then projected for the most plausible set of assumptions.

All impacts are calculated as *additions* to what would be the case if current policies were continued unchanged to 2010. The report contains detailed projections by four disaggregations: tenure (owner versus renter), age of household head (65-74, 75-84, 85^{+}), income quartile, and household type (single male, husband-wife family etc.). For each of these disaggregations housing attributes are tabulated, including building type, number of units in structure, length of residence in unit, size of unit, size of structure, and whether the household is receiving housing assistance.

The projected impacts of four policy alternatives are examined, summarized in the table at the top of the next page.

EXPANDED HOUSING ALLOWANCE PROGRAM FOR RENTERS

The major housing assistance programs currently in effect for which low-income elderly are eligible are housing allowance type programs. These are not entitlement programs and participation is limited. One obvious way of increasing housing assistance would be to expand the

IMPACTS ON HOUSING OF PARTICIPANTS AND COSTS OF DIFFERENT POLICY OPTIONS IN 2010

Program	Total Annual Subsidy ($Billions)[a]	Number of Participants (Millions)	Percentage of Participants Having Housing Problem Eliminated by Program: Structural Deficiency	Maintenance Deficiency	Excess Cost Burden
Rental voucher	3.3	1.50	14.3[b]	6.4[b]	89.0[b]
Owner voucher	5.2	2.76	26.7[b]	7.9[b]	29.6[b]
Reverse annuity mortgage	----	0.67	4.8	1.2	7.3
Congregate voucher	1.2	0.65	18.7[b]	8.2[b]	38.2[b]

a. 1984 dollars.
b. Since housing vouchers require that participants live in units meeting minimum standards of quality and affordability, the percentage of these problems removed depends on the percentage of participating households with the problems initially.

existing programs for renters. The policy option chosen for simulation is expanding the current U.S. Department of Housing and Urban Development (HUD) housing voucher program to cover a) all income-eligible households, b) eligible households that spend excessive amounts of their incomes (more than 30 percent) on housing, and c) eligible households that occupy units with structural or maintenance deficiencies.

Additional participation in the year 2010 under such expansion would range from 1.5 million for the entitlement version down to 200,000 under the version targeted on households in units with maintenance deficiencies. The total annual subsidy for the entitlement version is estimated at $3.3 billion (in addition to the subsidy if the current program were continued unchanged). The program is projected to reduce by more than 200,000 the number of elderly households living in units with structural deficiencies and by more than 100,000 the number in units with maintenance deficiencies. It would eliminate the excess cost burden otherwise being paid by 1.34 million elderly households.

VOUCHERS FOR HOME OWNERS

Home owners have not been eligible to participate in housing allowance programs in the United States. The reason for this may be that the emphasis on homeownership assistance is on helping households become homeowners. It would be straightforward to design a voucher program for owners, however, which takes home equity into account. The report simulates the impact of such a program with the same basic features and eligibility conditions as the expanded rental voucher option.

Under the entitlement option of homeowner vouchers, about 2.8 million households are projected to participate. Both of the nonentitlement versions are projected to be much smaller, with about 700,000 households participating. The total subsidy for homeowner vouchers is projected to be $5.2 million.

Vouchers for home owners would achieve larger reductions in structural and maintenance deficiencies than expanded vouchers for renters, but would remove the excess cost burden from somewhat fewer elderly households. This is primarily because, among the elderly, renters are a poorer group than homeowners.

EXPANDED AVAILABILITY OF HOME EQUITY CONVERSION MORTGAGES (HECMs)

For most elderly households the equity in their home represents the majority of their net worth, and the vast majority of these homeowners have eliminated the mortgage debt on their homes. This equity is seldom drawn down, however, largely because it has been difficult to access without having to sell one's home. In the past few years, new financial instruments in the form of HECMs have been developed to permit the elderly to use their equity for current expenses while continuing to live in their own homes. The report explores the income-generating potential of expanded use of HECMs, and estimates the effect of this additional income on the housing situation of the elderly in 2010.

Expanded availability of HECMs would achieve little improvement in housing conditions of the elderly. This is because HECMs free up additional money to meet personal needs, but beneficiary households will spend little of it on upgrading their housing.

CONGREGATE HOUSING VOUCHERS

Studies suggest that 12 to 60 percent of the frail elderly currently living in nursing homes could reside in the community if they receive appropriate, primarily nonmedical, supportive services. Congregate housing can serve just such a function. The report simulates the impact of a congregate housing voucher program with the same income eligibility criteria as the current rental voucher program, and eligibility further restricted to households with a head or spouse with activity limitations.

Such vouchers would have smaller effects than other voucher programs but larger effects than HECMs. However, they would have a greater effect than indicated by numbers alone. They would help the households most in need of upgraded housing if they are to avoid institutionalization.

Congregate housing vouchers also have considerable appeal. They would be directed to the functionally impaired, who are predominantly the elderly, without having to be another categorical program restricted to the elderly. They would also constitute an "existing" housing program because congregate facilities are privately financed and developed, and would be open to unsubsidized as well as subsidized households.

Chapter One

POLICY CONTEXT, METHODOLOGY, AND DATA

The American population is aging. As it ages, the needs of the elderly will grow as a proportion of society's needs, and a large share of the resources to meet those needs must come from the declining proportion of the population that is of working age. This phenomenon, combined with the fiscal stringency that will continue to be imposed on the economy because of the need to control and reduce the federal budget deficit, places a high premium on meeting the needs of the elderly in the most efficient way. One major area for which careful planning is needed is housing. The amount and types of housing needed by the elderly, as well as what they can afford, are influenced by their tendency to have, among other things, lower incomes, a greater number of activity limitations, and a higher incidence of living alone compared to younger households.

Wise choices among competing policy alternatives can only be made if there is good information. Little information has been available so far on which to base housing policy decisions for the future. This report helps to fill this gap by using microsimulation techniques to project what the elderly population will look like early in the next century, what their housing circumstances will be if policies continue unchanged, and what effects a range of alternative policies is likely to have on those circumstances.

Microsimulation is a powerful technique that allows analysts to use data bases with detailed information on the characteristics of individual households or persons to project the likely characteristics of the population in the future, and to estimate the likely effects of different policies on that population. Since the future cannot be known with certainty, the projections rest on a number of assumptions about economic, population, and other trends. The resulting estimates, of course, are only as good as the assumptions on which they are based. For this reason we have also tested alternative assumptions about living arrangements and housing preferences of our future elderly. If changing the assumptions makes relatively little difference to the estimates, the projections can be interpreted with more confidence than if the estimates vary widely.

The rest of this chapter briefly sets the policy context and provides an overview of the methodology and data used in the study. Chapter 2 describes the main characteristics of the elderly population projected for the year 2010 and presents the housing profile of America's elderly if the housing policies currently in effect continue unchanged under a baseline scenario and under alternative sets of assumptions about housing preferences and living arrangements. Chapters 3 through 6 then compare the impacts of four different policy alternatives on this profile. Chapter 7 concludes the report by comparing the four alternatives with one another.

POLICY CONTEXT

The aging of America is a well-recognized fact. Between 1985 and 2010, the population over 65 years of age will increase from 22 to 39 million--a growth rate of 77 percent compared to 32 percent for the population as a whole. The population over 75 years of age will more than double (from 8.5 to 19 million). The number of elderly households also will grow substantially, though not as rapidly because elderly households will increase in size as more married couples live longer before one of them dies. Beyond the year 2010 this aging will accelerate as the baby boom generation retires. The growth and aging of U.S. households is shown in figure 1.1. The youngest age group (under 35 years old)

FIGURE 1.1
GROWTH AND AGING OF U.S. POPULATION,
1985-2010

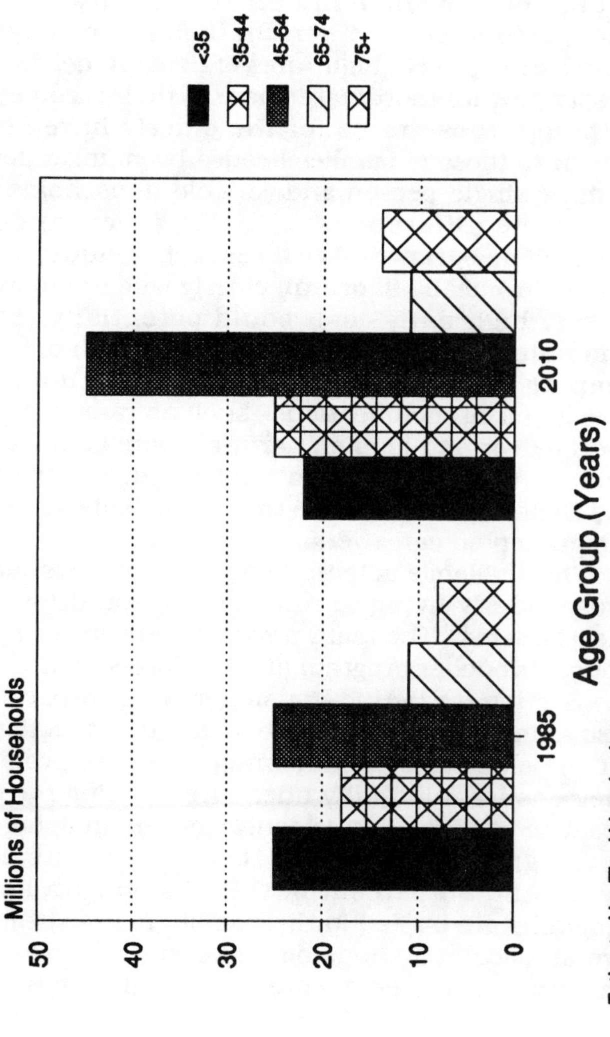

Estimated by The Urban Institute

will shrink in absolute size between 1985 and 2010. The 45-64 year old group will grow by 80 percent as the baby boom approaches retirement. The oldest age group (75 and over) will nearly double.

The stakes in the effort to develop successful housing policies for the elderly are enormous. The housing issue has two major dimensions: affordability and general housing quality on the one hand and suitability for elderly with impairments on the other. In the past, elderly households have had relatively high rates of living in deficient units and of spending an inordinate share of their incomes for shelter. Although these rates for the elderly have become more similar to those of families headed by younger persons, shifts to more single-person and very old households could again widen the differences, creating an expanded need for housing assistance. With respect to housing suitability, many chronically ill or frail elderly who are institutionalized at very high daily cost, could potentially remain in the community if less costly solutions--which are also more in keeping with their preferences--were made available. Dwelling unit modifications--such as ramps, grab bars, and special door and kitchen hardware--are an important part of such solutions. Modifications can help impaired persons use their homes, increase their independence, and decrease the burden on caregivers.

The challenge is to find policies that assist and stimulate those elderly living in unfavorable conditions to upgrade their housing. The main programs currently in place are the housing voucher program and its closely related counterpart, the Section 8 existing housing subsidy program. (There is also a limited volume of subsidized construction of housing for the elderly.) The advantage of these programs is that they ensure minimally adequate housing for participants because participation is contingent upon living in adequate housing; they also ensure that participants do not spend more than 30 percent of their income on housing. The programs are limited in their ability to assist the elderly who live in inadequate housing, however, for two reasons. First, only low-income renters are eligible; since most of the elderly own their own homes, this is a major restriction. Second, even among low-income renters, the current programs are not entitlement programs, and many of the elderly renters who live in inadequate housing are not able to participate even though they are eligible.

Expanding the rental voucher program into a low-income entitlement program would help more low-income elderly renters, but it would still fail to reach the homeowners in need. Extending housing vouchers to cover low-income homeowners is one policy option. This would ensure minimum housing standards for participants in the same way as the current program for renters because adequate housing would be a condition of participation, but it would considerably expand public expenditures on assisted housing.

Another alternative is to facilitate elderly homeowners use of the equity built up in their homes. In an effort to increase the resources available to elderly homeowners, most of whom have the bulk of their equity tied up in their homes, a new type of loan instrument has been developed, called a Home Equity Conversion Mortgage (HECM). Very few HECMs have been issued so far. If the use of HECMs were expanded, more homeowners might be able to upgrade their housing and lower their housing expense burden. The issue, of course, is whether they would choose to use their released funds on housing, rather than on other items they need.

As noted, with more of our population becoming elderly, increasing numbers of the elderly will need housing modifications if they are to continue living in the community. HECMs could conceivably be used to finance such modifications. However, a more direct means of providing housing with modifications that facilitate independent living would be a voucher program to subsidize living in congregate housing. Such a voucher program could be made available to both owners and renters as long as they meet an impairment criterion of eligibility.

To explore the potential of alternative housing policies, the effects of four policy alternatives are simulated:

- expansion of the housing voucher program for low-income elderly renters,

- housing vouchers for low-income elderly homeowners,

- greater use of Home Equity Conversion Mortgages among low-income homeowners, and

- implementation of a congregate housing voucher program for low-income elderly with activity limitations.

METHODOLOGY AND DATA

The microsimulation technique used to derive our estimates for the year 2010 allows us to use information on individual households from the Current Population Survey (CPS) to simulate the effects of many factors on the national population of elderly households. Our analysis is able to trace the effects of specific policy alternatives on housing circumstances, taking into account:

- fertility and mortality projections between now and 2010,

- overall economic growth projections for that period,

- the impact of federal income support policies (including Social Security),

- the housing preferences of the generation (now in middle and late middle age) that will *be* America's elderly in 2010, and

- the indirect effects resulting from the interaction of various determinants of housing circumstances.

Microsimulation with the Transfer Income Model

The specific microsimulation model used for the analysis the Transfer Income Model, called TRIM2, developed by The Urban Institute. TRIM2 is the latest in a family of static microsimulation models and is primarily used for policy analysis in the area of government tax and income transfer programs.[1] The model can use a person, family, or household as the unit of analysis. In this report, the unit of analysis is the household as defined by the Census Bureau.

TRIM2 is most often run with the March CPS data files. These CPS files are advantageous because they provide extensive demographic and income information on households and individuals. The CPS contains approximately 60,000 household records and 70,000 records of families or unrelated individuals, which when weighted are representative of the noninstitutional U.S. population.

To produce estimates for future years, TRIM2 "ages" the input data base by adjusting the sampling weights to reflect growth and change in the population, by adjusting labor force variables to reflect changes in unemployment, and by adjusting dollar amounts to reflect inflation and real economic growth. We have employed Census population projections for the year 2010 as the population targets in the TRIM2 aging procedure.[2] Projections of the number of households by age of head of household and household type for the year 2000 were taken from other Census work and projected to 2010 (see appendix C).

The file was also adjusted for projected macroeconomic trends using the macroeconomic model developed by Data Resources, Inc. Of the many pieces of the macroeconomic forecasts used, the most significant are projections of the long-run rate of economic growth and long-run unemployment rate. Table 1.1 gives the values of selected parameters over the projection period. A glance at these values indicates that DRI forecasts a fairly upbeat economic future for the United States over the next two decades,

TABLE 1.1 AVERAGE ANNUAL GROWTH IN SELECTED ECONOMIC FACTORS: 1985-2010 (percentages)

Consumer Price Index	5.5
Income by Source:[a]	
Wages and salaries	7.4
Non-farm proprietors' income	5.7
Personal dividend income	7.3
Personal interest income	7.4

Source: Appendix D.
a. This is growth in nominal income.

compared to the past ten years. (The aging process and the economic assumptions are detailed in appendices C and D.)

Additional Housing Data

Although the CPS contains some information on the housing circumstances of the households surveyed, the extent of these data is less than sufficient for exploring many central housing issues. The CPS contains the following housing information: tenure (unit occupied for cash rent, occupied rent free, or owner-occupied); type of dwelling (home, apartment, mobile home, group quarters, or hotel); the number of housing units in the structure; whether the household has lived in the unit five years or more; and, whether the unit is in a public housing project or the household receives some other form of assistance with its housing. We used information from the 1978 Annual Housing Survey (AHS) and the 1981 Survey of Residential Finance (SRF) to augment the Aged CPS file created by TRIM2 (see table 1.2).[3] Note that in addition to strictly housing attributes, we added a few variables regarding the

TABLE 1.2 HOUSING VARIABLES ADDED TO THE CPS FILE

General
- ratio of out-of-pocket housing expenses to income
- presence of structural deficiencies
- presence of maintenance deficiencies
- equity holdings in property
- number of stories in structure[a]
- number of rooms in unit[b]

Dwelling Modifications
- presence of household head with activity limitation; in husband-wife households, presence of spouse with activity limitation
- presence of minor dwelling modifications
- presence of major dwelling modifications

a. In properties containing 3 or more units.
b. Excludes bathrooms and kitchen.

presence of activity limitations of the household head and spouse (table 1.2). A series of predictive functions was used to assign values for the additional housing attributes to each household on the Aged CPS file.

Table 1.3 summarizes the functions estimated and used to predict variable values to append to the records in the Aged CPS file. Each column in the table represents a function, and the variable at the top of a column is the dependent variable in that function. Many of the dependent variables are dichotomous (i.e., taking on only the values of zero and one) and the equations for these are interpreted as probability functions. So, for example, predicted values derived from the equation for "stories" (i.e., the number of floors in a structure containing three or more units) are interpreted as the probability that a dwelling in a multi-unit building will be in a structure with four or more stories. The variables listed in the left column are the independent variables. The order in which the functions (columns) were estimated and applied in the predictions is read from left to right.

TABLE 1.3 PREDICTIVE EQUATIONS ESTIMATED FOR ADDING AHS VARIABLES TO THE CPS (dependent variables are at column heads; estimated in the order listed; "X" indicates a variable included in the equation)

Independent Variables	Stories[a]	Rooms[b,e]	No Mortgage Debt	Housing Exp./ Income>.3[e]	Structural Defects	Maintenance Defects	House Value[f,g]	Home Equity/ Value[c,f,h]	Head Limitations	Spouse Limitations	Minor Dwelling Mod.[e]	Major Dwelling Mod.[e]
Predicted Variables												
number of stories 4+=1[a]				x			x				x	x
number of rooms=1[b,e]				x			x					
no debt on home=1[f]				x								
housing expenses/income>.3=1[e]											x	x
structural defects=1[e]							x					
maintenance defects=1[e]						x						
house value[f,g]												
home equity/value[c,f,h]											x	x
head has activity limit.=1											x	x
spouse has activity limit.=1												
Other Variables												
age of household head	x	x	x	x	x	x	x	x	x			
age of spouse (if present)							x			x		
head is female=1	x	x	x	x	x	x	x		x			
number of adults		x	x		x	x	x					
head is black=1			x	x	x	x	x	x	x	x		
head has finished high school=1				x			x		x	x		
total household income	x	x	x		x	x	x		x	x	x	x
region of country	x	x	x	x	x	x	x	x	x	x		
located in SMSA	x	x	x	x	x	x	x	x	x	x		
head has employment income=1									x			
spouse has employment income=1				x						x		
dwelling type		x		x	x	x	x				x	x
units in structure	x										x	x
unit is subsidized=1[d]		x		x	x	x					x	x
in unit 5+ years=1		x	x	x	x	x		x				

a. Only for 3+ unit strucs.
b. 7+ rooms for owners/5+ rooms for renters.
c. For homes with debt.
d. Rental units only.
e. Estimated separately by tenure.
f. Owners only.
g. Separate estimate for mobile homes.
h. Estimated with Survey of Residential Finance data; estimated separately by different unit types.

In general, the objective in developing the predictive equations was to maximize predictive power, rather than to construct functions consistent with certain predefined behavioral models. Indeed, most of the functions can be thought of as loose combinations of housing demand functions and functions used to decompose house values or rents (so-called hedonic indices). This combination is especially evident in the models that include standard demand factors, like income and demographic variables, and certain housing attributes. For example, the fourth function--that for the ratio of housing expenses to income being greater than 0.3, the value above which housing expenses are defined to be excessive in federal housing legislation--contains demand variables and variables for the number of stories in the structure and the number of rooms in a unit. A more detailed explanation of the estimated functions is presented in appendix A, and some further description of the home equity variable is in appendix E.

We elected to define two separate variables to indicate dwelling quality, one indicating the presence of structural defects and the other indicating the presence of maintenance deficiencies. This decision is based on an analysis of trends in the dwelling quality of the elderly from 1974 to 1979 which showed that incidence of structural problems was declining but that of maintenance problems was increasing (Struyk and Turner 1984). The functions for these variables were estimated separately for owners and renters. (Table E.3 in appendix E contains the definitions of structural and maintenance deficiencies used throughout this report.)

There is also a set of functions predicting the likelihood that the head of the household or the spouse (if any) will have activity limitations. We chose to focus on activity limitations rather than health problems for two reasons. First, earlier analysis on the presence of compensating dwelling modifications revealed that activity limitations were much better predictors of the presence of such modifications than health status.[4] Second, past research suggests that individuals with activity limitations are more likely to live in units that make delivery of long-term care services more difficult (Newman 1985). The particular variables included in the models are based on an analysis of the demographic factors associated with the presence of activity limitations using data from the Health Interview Survey (Soldo 1983). The variables predicted for the presence of these various limitations are used in predicting the presence of two types of dwelling modification: minor (e.g., grab bars and changes to compensate for hearing and seeing problems), and major (e.g., ramps and bathrooms modified for wheelchair use). Separate functions were estimated for homeowners and renters.

With all the variables described above appended to the file, we have a file for 2010 which contains the following information for each household: a weight which properly represents the household in the population of households in 2010; information on the type of household and the demographic characteristics of the household members, including whether the head of household and spouse have activity limitations; data on the household's income and whether it receives various types of government assistance including Social Security, SSI, and housing assistance; information on the type of housing unit occupied, including the presence of dwelling deficiencies; data on the share of income devoted to housing; and, for homeowners, the value of equity held in the home.

Key Assumptions

Several important assumptions underlie the results presented. First, we have assumed that without any change in government housing programs, the proportion of elderly renters receiving housing assistance will be the same as is presently the case--a sanguine assumption in light of current federal budgetary woes. Second, we have assumed that the housing market will produce units consistent with the preferences of housing consumers. Because housing developers have responded with amazing alacrity to shifts in housing preferences in the past, this is probably a good assumption. Finally, it is assumed that housing costs and home equity holdings increase proportionately as real household incomes rise over the period.

Two additional assumptions apply to the "base case" scenario in the next chapter. The first of these is that the Census Bureau's middle-of-the-road projection is applicable, especially with respect to living arrangements (i.e., the number of persons living alone, the number of married couples, etc.). The second assumption involves what the housing preferences of the elderly will be in the future. Our base case assumption is that the housing preferences of persons with particular characteristics will remain the same between now and 2010. For example, a white, husband-wife household living in the urban northeast in 2010, with the head of household aged 70 and an annual household income of $20,000, is assumed to occupy the same type of housing that a household with exactly the same characteristics does now. Note that this does not prevent the distribution of housing attributes from changing. To the extent that the household composition, location, economic position, and racial composition of the elderly change over the period--as they do in the TRIM aging process--changes in the housing stock occupied by elderly households will take place.

Caveats in Interpreting the Results

Because so many factors are involved--and so many assumptions must be made about how the factors affect one another over the next two decades--the projected figures should be viewed as offering general orders of magnitude, rather than specific numerical estimates. Note that we do not claim to "predict" the future. Microsimulation allows the forecasting of future characteristics given an initial distribution of characteristics for a population and explicit assumptions about changes in that distribution. It will automatically carry along some of the complex relationships observed to exist among variables in the original data set, but it does not foresee changes in trends unless explicitly instructed to do so. In general, the overall approach has its greatest value for comparative analysis, particularly those contrasting a "base case"--like that presented in the next chapter--with alternative outcomes resulting from different policy interventions.

These qualifications notwithstanding, the projections presented in this report provide useful information to policymakers. On one hand, the estimates of the situation without policy changes show how housing preferences and current policies are likely to affect the future housing situation of the elderly. On the other hand, the simulated impacts of alternative policy interventions can help policymakers evaluate alternative policies dealing with the housing problems that will be experienced by elderly households in the future.

Notes, chapter one

1. For a general introduction to TRIM see Sulvetta (1976). TRIM2 was designed as a generalized framework for microsimulation that could be adapted to subject areas other than income transfers or to units of analysis other than households. For example, given a database describing individual corporations within a state, TRIM2 could be used to simulate state corporate income taxes. For a more detailed description of the use of TRIM2 in the analysis reported here, see Katsura, Struyk, and Newman (1988).

2. The Census Bureau provides three alternative population projections which differ in the assumptions made regarding fertility and mortality. The middle path assumes a total fertility rate of 1.9 births per woman and life expectancy in 2050 of 76.7 years. See U.S. Bureau of the Census (1986).

3. The 1978 AHS included about 70,000 records and had a special Housing Modification Supplement. The 1981 SRF was part of the 1980 Census and included about 62,000 nonfarm, privately owned residential properties.

4. For details see Struyk and Katsura (1985), Struyk (1982).

Chapter Two

PROJECTED CHANGES IN THE CHARACTERISTICS AND HOUSING SITUATION OF THE ELDERLY POPULATION IF CURRENT POLICIES CONTINUE

This chapter begins with a profile of how the population of households is projected to change between 1985 and 2010. A detailed description of how the housing circumstances of elderly households will change over the 25-year projection period under the base case assumptions just noted in chapter 1 follows. The chapter ends by comparing the base case projections with projections estimated under alternative assumptions about living arrangements and housing preferences.

PROJECTED CHANGES IN THE CHARACTERISTICS OF U.S. HOUSEHOLDS

The changes projected in the distribution of households among household types and in the age of household heads are shown in table 2.1. Several points stand out. First, over the period there is likely to be a major decline--almost 8 percentage points--in the percentage of households headed by a married couple. By the end of the period, such households will constitute only 50 percent of all households, down from 58 percent. All other types of households will increase in relative importance, but the biggest gain is projected to be among males living alone. Second, a very large drop is projected in the number of households headed by a person under age 35, from 29.2 to 18.9 percent of all households, caused by the aging of the baby boom cohort. The compensating increase will be among those in the 45-64

TABLE 2.1 DISTRIBUTION OF HOUSEHOLDS BY HOUSEHOLD TYPE AND AGE OF HEAD: 1985 AND 2010 (percentages)

	1985	2010
Household Type		
Husband-wife	58.0	50.1
Male-headed families	2.6	3.4
Female-headed families	11.7	12.0
Male individual	12.3	16.6
Female individual	15.5	17.9
Age of Household Head		
Under 35	29.2	18.9
35-44	20.1	21.1
45-64	29.7	38.7
65-74	12.6	9.3
75+	8.5	12.0

Source: Tabulations of 1985 CPS file and Aged TRIM2 file.

age group. Among households headed by someone 65 years of age or older, the percentage of households in the 65-74 age group will actually decline (the absolute number of households in this group will even decline slightly). In contrast, the share of households over age 75 is projected to increase substantially, to 12 percent of all households in 2010.[1]

Some additional detail on these changes is provided in table 2.2. Concentrating on the pattern for households headed by an elderly person, we see a marked increase in the share of elderly households anticipated to be headed by married couples, reflecting primarily the increased life expectancy of men. There will be corresponding reductions in the percentage of female-headed households and females living alone.

Finally, the changes in household incomes expected over the period are shown in table 2.3. The ratios of incomes in 2010 to those in 1984 show the change in real incomes.[2]

TABLE 2.2 DISTRIBUTION OF HOUSEHOLDS BY HOUSEHOLD TYPE FOR SELECTED AGE GROUPS: 1985-2010 (percentages)

	Husband-wife	Male Head	Female Head	Male Individual	Female Individual
Age 35-44					
1985	66.4	2.9	14.6	10.5	5.6
2010	53.1	4.3	13.8	20.7	8.1
Age 45-64					
1985	65.9	2.7	10.5	8.5	12.4
2010	59.2	3.5	11.5	13.7	12.1
Age 65-74					
1985	52.0	1.6	7.2	8.8	30.3
2010	53.8	1.3	4.9	10.8	29.2
Age 75+					
1985	33.8	1.6	9.1	10.9	44.6
2010	36.9	.9	6.2	11.8	44.2

TABLE 2.3 CHANGES IN MEAN REAL HOUSEHOLD INCOME BY TYPE OF HOUSEHOLD: 1984-2010

Age of Household Head	1984	Ratio: 2010/1984
Under 35	$24,100	1.16
35-44	33,400	1.26
45-64	33,250	1.24
65-74	20,600	1.13
75+	15,000	1.08

Source: Tabulations of the 1985 CPS file and the Aged TRIM2 file for 2010.

There is a small overall increase, with households in each age of household head category experiencing some income growth. Given the assumption that Social Security will not rise in real terms, the incomes of the elderly on average will rise slightly less rapidly than those of younger households.

HOUSING NEEDS OF THE ELDERLY IN 2010 UNDER THE BASE CASE

In 2010 the population of households headed by a person age 65 or older is projected to consist of about 25.1 million households, compared to about 18.2 million such households in 1985--an increase of 38 percent.[3] We describe the housing situation of the elderly in 2010 relative to 1978[4] through a series of twelve tables, divided into three groups based on the housing information they contain. The first set deals with general housing characteristics; the second with the incidence of activity limitations and the presence of compensating dwelling modifications; and the third with the incidence of physical deficiencies in the units occupied, the share of income devoted to housing, and the amount of home equity accumulated by homeowners. For each of these three aspects of the housing situation, tables are presented for four disaggregations:

- tenure (owners vs. renters),
- age of household head (65-74, 75-85, 85+),
- income quartiles, and
- five household types.

We should note at the outset that an overall increase in the rate of homeownership among the elderly is projected from 73 percent in 1978 to 76 percent in 2010. This increase is projected to affect nearly all groups. Since many other housing attributes--ranging from the share of income devoted to housing to the type of dwelling occupied--are associated with tenure choice, this shift has consequences for the other results.

General Housing Attributes

The general housing attributes discussed in this section encompass type of structure, whether the household in the unit receives housing assistance, and size of unit.

Type of Structure. The traditional house or apartment will remain in favor over the next quarter century if households' preferences remain fixed (tables 2.4A-2.4D), and there will be little shift to mobile homes or other living situations (such as boarding houses or hotels).[5]

More change is evident in the type of units occupied. Overall, the share of households in single unit structures rises by about 2.1 percentage points over the period, consistent with the increase in homeownership. There is a sharp decline in the share of households occupying units in 2-4 unit structures and a small rise in those living in large (10+ unit) structures. Most of the change is due to changes among renters for which a 9.5 percentage point shift from 1-4 unit structures to larger structures occurs. The situation of owners changes relatively little.

The projected shift to larger structures is particularly evident for certain subgroups. Older households--especially those headed by a person over 85--comprise one such group. Other groups include women living alone and households in the lowest income quartile. Piecing these facts together, one sees a shift of low-income, older old women who live alone moving to large rental buildings.[6]

Housing Assistance. The pattern of renters shifting into larger units is consistent with the findings for renter households who will receive housing assistance payments. The consistency arises because many of the buildings in

TABLE 2.4A GENERAL HOUSING ATTRIBUTES BY TENURE IN 1978 AND 2010 (percentages)

	All Households		Owners		Renters[d]	
	1978	2010	1978	2010	1978	2010
Building type						
house/apartment	93.5	93.4	92.4	92.4	96.5	96.9
mobile home	5.8	6.0	7.6	7.5	1.0	1.2
other	.7	.6	.1	.1	2.5	1.9
Number of units in structure						
1	71.4	73.5	90.0	91.1	20.5	18.9
2-4	13.2	9.4	7.1	5.4	29.9	22.0
5-9	3.6	3.9	.7	.8	11.7	13.6
10+	11.8	13.1	2.2	2.7	37.9	45.5
Household has lived in unit 5 years or more	77.3	85.4	86.1	92.2	53.3	64.2
Household receiving housing assistance[a]	21.2	30.8	--	--	21.2	30.8
Large Unit[b]	18.7	15.2	18.6	14.4	19.0	17.6
Unit in 4+ story structure[c]	6.9	6.5	1.4	1.2	21.7	21.5

a. Renters only.
b. 5 or more rooms for renters; 7 or more for owners.
c. Only for structures with 3+ units. d. Cash renters only.

which elderly households receiving housing assistance reside are very large structures.If in the future the kinds of elderly households which currently receive assistance continue to be assisted at the same rates as they do now, there will be a substantial increase in the percentage of renters receiving assistance--from 21 to 31 percent. The oldest households do not share in this increase; indeed the largest increase is for those households headed by a person aged 75-84. It is not

TABLE 2.4B GENERAL HOUSING ATTRIBUTES BY AGE IN 1978 AND 2010 (percentages)

	65-74		75-84		85+	
	1978	2010	1978	2010	1978	2010
Building type						
house/apartment	93.1	92.8	94.0	93.8	94.9	94.8
mobile home	6.3	6.8	5.1	5.6	4.3	3.8
other	.6	.4	.9	.6	.8	1.4
Number of units in structure						
1	73.7	77.7	67.2	70.8	69.8	67.4
2-4	12.6	9.4	14.3	9.4	13.3	10.1
5-9	3.2	3.6	4.3	4.0	4.4	5.1
10+	10.5	9.4	14.2	15.9	12.4	17.4
Household has lived in unit 5 years or more	74.9	82.9	80.7	87.1	84.4	88.4
Household receiving housing assistance[a]	20.0	25.0	21.2	36.3	26.2	26.5
Large Unit	19.8	19.7	16.8	11.4	17.2	12.7
Unit in 4+ story structure	6.0	4.5	8.2	7.2	8.3	8.8

a. Renters only.

clear why the oldest households (who continue to live outside of institutions) participate at lower rates; it may be that this reflects the reluctance of very old persons to participate in "welfare programs" generally.

The household type with the largest increase in the percentage receiving housing assistance is women living alone--from 26 to 39 percent. Men living alone experience the second greatest rise, but this is only about one-third as great as that for women living alone. The proportion of

TABLE 2.4C GENERAL HOUSING ATTRIBUTES BY HOUSEHOLD TYPE IN 1978 AND 2010 (percentages)

	Husband-wife Only		Husband-wife w/Others		Female Alone		Male Alone		Others	
	1978	2010	1978	2010	1978	2010	1978	2010	1978	2010
Building type										
house/apartment	92.3	92.6	97.8	97.4	93.5	94.2	90.2	91.4	96.8	94.6
mobile home	7.5	7.3	2.1	2.6	5.8	5.1	5.8	6.6	3.1	3.1
other	.2	.1	.1	.0	.7	.7	4.0	2.0	.1	.1
Number of units in structure										
1	82.1	84.5	85.3	89.7	59.1	62.4	58.5	62.8	76.9	79.2
2-4	8.6	6.8	8.9	7.5	18.2	12.5	14.8	9.7	14.0	9.7
5-9	1.9	1.8	1.6	.9	5.3	5.8	6.1	7.0	3.4	3.4
10+	7.4	6.9	4.2	1.9	17.5	20.4	20.6	20.5	5.7	7.7
Household has lived in unit 5 years or more	78.6	88.0	82.1	88.2	76.1	83.4	67.7	82.1	82.1	83.9
Household receiving housing assistance[a]	14.1	18.0	11.6	9.8	25.9	39.4	22.0	26.3	13.4	15.3
Large Unit	19.1	16.2	34.1	63.4	13.5	5.7	12.1	5.5	28.8	37.0
Unit in 4+ story structure	4.8	4.0	2.6	1.7	10.3	8.6	9.7	8.7	3.1	4.9

a. Renters only.

TABLE 2.4D GENERAL HOUSING ATTRIBUTES BY INCOME QUARTILE IN 1978 AND 2010 (percentages)

	Lowest Quartile		2nd Quartile		3rd Quartile		Highest Quartile	
	1978	2010	1978	2010	1978	2010	1978	2010
Building type								
house/apartment	92.3	94.1	92.7	91.7	91.7	92.8	96.1	95.3
mobile home	6.5	5.2	6.4	7.6	7.6	6.8	3.6	4.4
other	1.3	.7	.9	.9	.7	.4	.3	.3
Number of units in structure								
1	63.3	61.3	67.8	73.0	75.5	77.6	78.5	81.6
2-4	16.7	11.8	15.6	9.9	11.4	8.8	9.4	7.4
5-9	4.9	6.7	4.1	3.7	3.1	3.0	2.5	2.4
10+	15.2	20.2	12.5	13.3	9.9	10.7	9.7	8.6
Household has lived in unit 5 years or more	74.4	82.1	76.8	84.5	78.1	86.4	80.0	88.4
Household receiving housing assistance[a]	34.5	47.8	21.8	29.7	8.8	10.6	2.6	4.5
Large Unit	12.0	5.4	14.5	4.7	17.1	6.2	30.8	44.2
Unit in 4+ story structure	8.9	8.0	6.4	4.8	5.5	4.0	6.7	7.9

a. Renters only.

husband-wife households with others present who receive housing assistance will actually fall slightly. And as one would expect, households in the lowest income quartile will experience the largest rise in assistance.[7]

According to these projections, about 1.8 million elderly households will receive housing assistance in 2010, compared to about 1.4 million according to 1983 American Housing Survey data. The absolute level for 2010 does not appear to be large;[8] however, the rate of growth in the number of households receiving assistance seems very optimistic under current budget conditions, and would require a considerable expansion in housing assistance programs currently in operation.[9]

Size of Unit. There are some noteworthy findings regarding the size of the units occupied, as indicated by the number of rooms in the unit. We are using a simple cutoff of five rooms or more to identify a large rental dwelling unit, and seven rooms or more to indicate a large owner-occupied unit. A modest decrease in the share of all households occupying large units is anticipated for both homeowners and renters. There are, however, some groups that do experience increases. Husband-wife households with others present show a large increase. In addition, households in the highest income quartile are expected to occupy larger units--an increase from 31 to 44 percent of these households will be in such units.[10]

Activity Limitations and Dwelling Modifications

As noted by many housing analysts, the prevalence of activity limitations and the need for compensating features in the residence is one of the primary factors differentiating the housing needs of the elderly from those of younger households. The next set of tables (tables 2.5A-2.5D) presents estimates of the incidence of activity limitations and the incidence of compensating dwelling modifications for elderly households in 1978 and 2010. Although not

TABLE 2.5A ACTIVITY LIMITATIONS AND DWELLING MODIFICATIONS BY TENURE: 1978 AND 2010 (percentages)

	All Households		Owners		Renters	
	1978	2010	1978	2010	1978	2010
Activity Limitations						
Head	8.1	10.9	7.2	9.1	10.8	16.4
Spouse	2.6	4.0	2.9	4.4	1.7	2.6
Presence of Dwelling Modifications						
Major	2.8	3.3	1.7	2.2	5.5	6.6
Minor	6.2	7.4	6.0	7.3	6.6	7.8

TABLE 2.5B ACTIVITY LIMITATIONS AND DWELLING MODIFICATIONS BY AGE OF HOUSEHOLD HEAD: 1978 AND 2010 (percentages)

	65-74		75-84		85+	
	1978	2010	1978	2010	1978	2010
Activity Limitations						
Head	5.4	a	11.1	10.5	19.9	62.3
Spouse	2.2	0.3	3.1	5.0	3.6	15.5
Presence of Dwelling Modifications						
Major	2.2	0.3	3.5	2.6	5.1	20.2
Minor	4.7	a	7.6	7.4	13.0	41.2

a. Less than 0.1.

illustrated directly by the data in these tables, it is the case that many more elderly report such limitations than live in units that have special features to help cope with the problems.[11]

Activity Limitations. A clear increase over the period is projected in the percentage of households with the head or spouse with an activity limitation. This increase is presumably primarily attributable to the sharply increased share of all of the elderly who are over age 75. This point is reinforced by the pattern apparent in the figures in table 2.5B, which show a very sharp increase in the share of those over age 84 with an activity limitation. This rise is certainly attributable at least in part to the increased average age of those in this group. A decrease in the incidence of activity limitations among elderly households headed by a younger person is projected, especially for those in the 65-74 age bracket. Our view is that while this type of pattern may in fact develop over the next 25 years, the statistical approach used in assigning an activity disability to a household on the TRIM2 file very likely has accentuated the underlying pattern. In fact, the available analyses on trends in morbidity do not identify a clear pattern of increasing or decreasing morbidity among the very old.[12]

An interesting pattern in the incidence of activity limitations, again possibly accentuated in these estimates, is also evident for households according to their living arrangements (table 2.5C). Some reduction in the incidence of activity limitations for husband-wife households is projected, especially those in which other persons are also present. In contrast, women living alone and "other" households will have a particularly sharp increase in their incidence of activity limitations; for women, this presumably reflects the increased average age projected for this group.

Change is also evident in the incidence rates of activity limitations by household income. The rates will increase for households in the two lowest income quartiles; households in the lowest income quartile are predicted to have a

TABLE 2.5C ACTIVITY LIMITATIONS AND DWELLING MODIFICATIONS BY HOUSEHOLD TYPE: 1978 AND 2010 (percentages)

	Husband-wife Only		Husband-wife w/Others		Female Alone		Male Alone		Others	
	1978	2010	1978	2010	1978	2010	1978	2010	1978	2010
Activity Limitations										
Head	5.0	1.6	6.0	1.6	10.9	22.3	7.5	3.6	11.3	19.1
Spouse	5.8	9.4	5.9	4.8	--	--	--	--	--	--
Presence of Dwelling Modifications										
Major	2.2	2.3	2.1	2.1	3.2	4.3	2.6	0.5	3.1	7.8
Minor	5.4	1.3	5.6	1.3	7.2	14.2	4.5	2.8	6.6	15.8

TABLE 2.5D ACTIVITY LIMITATIONS AND DWELLING MODIFICATIONS BY INCOME GROUP: 1978 AND 2010 (percentages)

	Lowest Quartile		2nd Quartile		3rd Quartile		Highest Quartile	
	1978	2010	1978	2010	1978	2010	1978	2010
Activity Limitations								
Head	12.2	23.4	9.5	11.6	6.6	5.3	4.4	3.6
Spouse	1.2	2.6	2.8	6.9	3.5	4.3	2.8	2.1
Presence of Dwelling Modifications								
Major	3.5	3.1	2.7	3.5	2.3	2.1	2.5	4.3
Minor	7.7	13.6	5.9	9.2	5.7	3.8	5.3	3.1

doubling of the rate at which they experience these activity limitations. This increase may well stem from the fact that many households with higher incomes at the time of the onset of a serious activity limitation eventually "spend their way down" to a lower income level in the process of caring for the impaired person.

Dwelling Modifications. A modest increase in the incidence of major unit modifications is projected from 2.8 to 3.3 percent of all units occupied by elderly-headed households, and a somewhat larger increase for minor changes, from 6.2 to 7.4 percent. This trend is evident for both owner- and renter-occupied units.

One interesting point is that the increase will be dramatically greater for both major and minor modifications for those over age 84 than for the younger age groups among the elderly. This surge reflects the large increase projected in the proportion in the oldest age group with activity limitations.[13] Since the oldest households are concentrated among those with the lowest incomes, it is not surprising to find that these groups tend to exhibit higher than average rates of increase in occupancy of units with special features. The incidence of major modifications is expected to increase or stay the same for all other household types except males living alone. But women living alone and "other" households are the only groups projected to make more use of minor modifications. Of course, as noted earlier, these estimates assume that specially equipped units will be available for these households to occupy, an assumption that is far from certain.

Deficiencies and Housing Finance

Unit Deficiencies. The overall pattern with respect to dwelling unit deficiencies will be one of modest increases in structural deficiencies (from 9.4 to 12.1 percent of units occupied by the elderly) and a very small rise in maintenance deficiencies (2.2 to 2.3 percent).[14] For both types of deficiencies, the increase is projected to be greater for homeowners than for renters.

Further examination of the figures in Tables 2.6B-2.6D support the proposition that the projected rise in incidence in deficiencies is associated with demographic change. This is clearly evident in table 2.6B where one sees relatively little change in either type of deficiency for the youngest group of elderly households (aged 65-74). For the older-old, however, there will be a sharp increase, especially for structural deficiencies. This kind of pattern reflects a combination of incomes declining with age and the inability of older homeowners to do or supervise repairs on their units. As the population ages, this pattern, which has been observed in the past, is amplified.

The role of low income is also clearly supported by the data in table 2.6D, in which one sees a very high incidence of deficiencies for households in the lowest income quartile--incidence rates that are projected to increase sharply over the period. In contrast, the incidence of such problems will fall from lower levels for all households in the higher income quartiles. There is little change projected in the incidence of structural deficiencies for husband-wife households over the period, but a sharp increase for women living alone. Maintenance deficiencies will only increase for women living alone and "other" households.

Excessive Housing Expenditures. We define housing expenditures to be excessive when they exceed 30 percent of household income. A quick look at the figures in the second panel of table 2.6A reveals similar results for homeowners and renters: both groups are expected to experience a modest decline in the percentage of households with excessive expenditures.

The decline for homeowners is part of a larger picture. The increased life expectancy of men will lead not only to a higher rate of homeownership, but ownership by relatively well-to-do households. Moreover, this pattern will lead to longer tenure periods and hence a larger share of homeowners who occupy their homes without any mortgage debt (an increase from 87 to 92 percent over the period). The lack of mortgage debt, of course, is a very strong determinant of the share of income going to housing expenses.

With the elderly as a group consisting heavily of homeowners, the results for homeowners dominate the rest of the results reported in these tables. Females living alone and households in the "other" category are the only household types projected to have an increase in spending more than 30 percent of their incomes on housing. Even among the lowest income households, the results for homeowners and renters combined indicate a decline in the share of households spending an excessive share of income on housing. There is, however, another important factor at work for renters: the increase in housing assistance recipiency. Recall that by 2010 some 31 percent of renters are projected to be receiving assistance (up from 21 percent in the base year). Practically all of the households projected to be added to the assistance rolls would otherwise be spending over 30 percent of their incomes on housing. So the additional assistance has a major impact on the incidence of excessive housing expenditures by renters.

Home Equity. Lastly, the amount of equity that homeowners hold in their homes will be of great interest when we explore the possibilities for the Home Equity Conversion Mortgages in a later chapter.[15] Tables 2.6A - 2.6D show the distribution of equity using three value groups (1984 prices). The results for all homeowners (table 2.6A) indicate a greater clustering of values in the middle ($50,000-$90,000) category over the period caused primarily by reductions in the share of households in the lowest equity range.

Two sharp differences from the overall pattern are worthy of note. First, with respect to living arrangements, husband-wife households display a comparatively large shift from the lowest part of the equity distribution to the middle and upper segments; their average equity holdings clearly rise. For persons living alone, in contrast, the share in the highest

TABLE 2.6A DEFICIENCIES AND HOUSING FINANCES BY TENURE: 1978 AND 2010 (percentages)

	All Households		Owners		Renters	
	1978	2010	1978	2010	1978	2010
Presence of Dwelling Deficiencies						
Structural	9.4	12.1	8.8	11.7	11.0	13.3
Maintenance	2.2	2.3	1.6	1.8	3.6	3.6
Housing Expenditures Greater Than 30 Percent of Income	25.7	22.9	15.3	13.8	52.1	51.1
Home Equity Holdings[a]						
Under $50,000			46.5	34.1		
$50-90,000			35.9	48.7		
Over $90,000			17.7	17.3		
Percentage of Owners with no Mortgage Debt			87.2	91.7		

TABLE 2.6B DEFICIENCIES AND HOUSING FINANCE BY AGE OF HOUSEHOLD HEAD IN 1978 AND 2010 (percentages)

	65-74		75-84		85+	
	1978	2010	1978	2010	1978	2010
Presence of Dwelling Deficiencies						
Structural	9.1	10.1	9.8	13.5	10.3	14.8
Maintenance	2.2	2.3	2.0	2.1	2.3	2.9
Housing Expenditures Greater Than 30 Percent of Income	23.7	19.0	28.2	24.3	33.2	33.9
Home Equity Holdings[a]						
Under $50,000	44.2	31.1	49.6	36.5	54.2	36.7
$50-90,000	37.5	51.0	33.5	47.0	31.1	45.7
Over $90,000	18.3	17.9	16.9	16.5	14.7	17.7
Percentage of Owners With No Mortgage Debt	83.5	82.4	93.1	99.7	97.1	100.0

a. In 1984 dollars.

TABLE 2.6C DEFICIENCIES AND HOUSING FINANCES BY HOUSEHOLD TYPE IN 1978 AND 2010 (percentages)

	Husband-wife Only		Husband-wife w/Others		Female Alone		Male Alone		Other	
	1978	2010	1978	2010	1978	2010	1978	2010	1978	2010
Presene of Dwelling Deficiencies										
Strutural	5.7	6.5	10.1	9.1	8.7	16.5	19.2	18.2	15.2	13.7
Maintenance	1.0	.8	2.3	2.0	2.2	2.8	4.1	3.7	4.1	5.5
Housing Expenditures Greater Than 30 Percent of Income	14.8	4.7	13.3	7.1	40.5	44.7	29.6	16.7	18.6	30.1
Home Equity Holdings[a]										
Under $50,000	41.4	22.4	41.1	20.6	52.5	50.7	52.8	41.8	50.2	38.5
$50-90,000	38.0	55.4	36.3	42.2	34.2	42.8	32.9	48.8	33.8	38.4
Over $90,000	20.6	22.2	22.6	37.2	13.3	6.6	14.3	9.4	16.0	23.1
Percentage of Owners With No Mortgage Debt	85.6	90.3	71.2	65.8	93.0	97.7	91.6	95.8	87.6	91.1

a. In 1984 dollars.

TABLE 2.6D DEFICIENCIES AND HOUSING FINANCES BY INCOME QUARTILES IN 1978 AND 2010 (percentages)

	Lowest Quartile		2nd Quartile		3rd Quartile		Highest Quartile	
	1978	2010	1978	2010	1978	2010	1978	2010
Presence of Dwelling Deficiencies								
Structural	18.2	39.4	9.9	5.4	6.3	3.1	3.6	1.4
Maintenance	3.8	8.3	2.3	.4	1.7	.3	.9	.2
Housing Expenditures								
Greater Than 30 Percent of Income	54.4	49.8	34.1	27.1	13.4	11.8	2.2	3.6
Home Equity Holdings[a]								
Under $50,000	66.0	78.0	55.5	48.9	45.8	25.3	28.0	2.9
$50-90,000	25.5	20.6	33.7	48.9	38.1	67.6	42.0	48.7
Over $90,000	8.5	1.4	10.7	2.2	16.2	7.1	30.0	48.4
Percentage of Owners With No Mortgage Debt	91.2	95.8	91.1	97.1	88.2	94.5	80.5	82.0

a. In 1984 dollars.

equity category actually falls over the period, which reinforces clustering in the middle group; and the move out of the lowest segment is small relative to the move for husband-wife households. Second, the kind of differences just stated are repeated by income class, with lower income homeowners tending to have the same pattern as those living alone and the higher income homeowners resembling the husband-wife households. These findings suggest the possibilities for using HECMs will be no greater in the future than currently for many households, if our assumptions about the relationship between house values and income developments are reasonable.

A final comment on the results just presented on the housing circumstances of the elderly in the year 2010 seems in order. The process employed to generate these figures is complex and subject to various types of error along its several steps. While we believe that in general we have constructed a reasonable picture of the future, given the constant-preference and other assumptions we have made, we stress again that these are not predictions. They are estimates that were derived under particular assumptions, and their greatest utility will be in the analysis of the impact of housing policies that might be implemented in the next several years.

ALTERNATIVE PROJECTIONS

In this section we present the results of three additional simulations, employing alternative assumptions about developments in living arrangements and about the housing preferences of the future elderly. The complete set of projections can be characterized as follows:[16]

	Assumptions About:	
	Living Arrangements	Housing Preferences
Case 1	base case	base case
Case 2	alternative	base case
Case 3	base case	alternative
Case 4	alternative	alternative

Alternative Assumptions About Living Arrangements

The projections presented in the last section were based on the middle of three alternative demographic projections of households to the year 2000 developed by the Bureau of the Census (and extended to 2010 in our analysis). The three series primarily differ in the assumptions made about future trends in divorce and remarriage rates, the rate at which never-married people continue to live alone, and the rate at which young people continue to live at home. One of the alternatives to the middle series--Series A, the one we use in constructing our alternative projections--gives greater weight to the rates of divorce and changes in living arrangements that have occurred over the past 25 years.[17]

Compared to the middle series, the Series A projections yield a slightly higher number of elderly-headed households in 2000 (22.9 versus 22.6 million households). More importantly, the Series A projections possess a different distribution of the elderly among living arrangements in 2010 (see table 2.7). The greatest change in the alternative scenario is for female-headed families in which the head is 75 years of age or older, for which there is a 1.8 percentage point reduction. Most of these women are shifted to living alone, although some are in husband-wife households, a group which shows a modest increase among the very old (from 36.9 to 37.6 percent of all households). Overall, the largest increases are among those living alone--but even these changes are not large in absolute terms.

Alternative Assumptions About Housing Preferences

Several changes over the next 25 years in tastes and preferences for housing among the elderly are plausible: a shift to larger single-family homes for homeowners, renters increasingly concentrated in large housing complexes, or a general improvement in housing quality. In our judgment, the best guide to the housing preferences of the future

TABLE 2.7 DISTRIBUTION OF THE ELDERLY AMONG LIVING ARRANGEMENTS IN 2010, BASE CASE AND ALTERNATIVE (percentages)

Age/Case	Families: Husband-Wife	Families: Male Head	Families: Female Head	Individuals: Male	Individuals: Female
65-74					
Base	53.8	1.3	4.9	10.8	29.2
Alternative	53.8	1.0	3.8	11.6	29.8
75+					
Base	36.9	.9	6.2	11.8	44.2
Alternative	37.6	.6	4.4	11.6	45.6

Source: Tabulations from the Aged TRIM2 file.

elderly may well be the housing consumption of those who are now middle-aged. Our alternative assumption, therefore, is that the elderly in 2010 will have the housing preferences of households 25 years their junior in 1985. Mechanically, in the predictive models used to append housing variables to the Aged TRIM2 file, we reduced the age of each elderly household by 25 years.[18]

Only the preferences for some of the physical attributes of the unit have in fact been altered for our alternative: the number of rooms, the presence of various deficiencies, and number of stories in multi-unit structures. The presence of dwelling modifications and housing finances, particularly the share of income devoted to housing, are affected only to the degree that occupying a new type of unit causes them to change. For example, we know that, other things equal, larger units are associated with a higher incidence of households devoting an "excessive" share of their incomes to housing. To the extent that households shift to larger units, the incidence of high housing expenditures will rise. We have *not* changed the incidence of having paid off mortgages.

This surely differs between middle-aged and elderly households, but we have no strong reason to expect the life-cycle patterns to change.[19] We have not altered the incidence of activity limitations for the same reason.

Sensitivity of the Projections to the Changed Assumptions

The extent of change in the projected housing circumstances of the elderly resulting from the modifications of the assumptions about living arrangements and housing preferences is accurately characterized as modest. This can be illustrated with the results for the share of the elderly who are projected to be homeowners under the various cases, which are listed below:

case 1 (base case)	76 percent
case 2	75 percent
case 3	76 percent
case 4	75 percent

The slight drop between cases 1 and 3 compared to cases 2 and 4 is due to the increased importance of single-person households in the latter two cases. But as is clear from the figures, the impact on tenure rates is slight, since even a large share of single-person elderly are homeowners.

In looking at other results for the different cases, we focus on a few housing characteristics which either have exhibited some noticeable change or which are of particular policy importance. These include the presence of dwelling deficiencies, spending an excessive share of income on housing, and the level of equity holdings in owner-occupied housing. The results for these characteristics are organized in four tables (2.8 - 2.11), with the base case being case 1, the alternative living arrangements being case 2, and cases 3 and 4 adding changed housing preferences to cases 1 and 2, respectively. The effects of changing assumptions can be seen by contrasting results for cases 1 and 3 and those for cases 2 and 4. Since the shifts are quite similar, we

TABLE 2.8 SELECTED HOUSING ATTRIBUTES BY TENURE IN 2010 UNDER DIFFERENT ASSUMPTIONS (percentages)

	All Households				Owners				Renters			
	Case (1)	Case (2)	Case (3)	Case (4)	Case (1)	Case (2)	Case (3)	Case (4)	Case (1)	Case (2)	Case (3)	Case (4)
Large unit (1=yes)[a]	15.2	14.3	23.8	22.9	14.4	13.5	25.8	24.9	17.6	16.8	17.4	16.6
Number of units in structure												
1	73.5	73.1	73.5	73.1	91.1	91.0	91.0	91.0	18.9	18.6	18.9	18.6
2-4	9.4	9.5	9.4	9.5	5.4	5.4	5.4	5.4	22.0	21.8	22.0	21.8
5-9	3.9	4.0	3.9	4.0	.8	.8	.8	.8	13.6	13.7	13.6	13.7
10+	13.1	13.4	13.1	13.4	2.7	2.7	2.7	2.7	45.5	45.9	45.5	45.9
Unit has structural deficiency	12.1	12.1	10.7	10.7	11.7	11.8	11.6	11.6	13.3	13.2	8.0	8.0
Unit has maintenance deficiency	2.3	2.2	2.8	2.7	1.8	1.8	2.5	2.5	3.6	3.4	3.5	3.3
Household spends over 30% of income on housing (1=yes)	22.9	22.9	23.1	23.0	13.8	13.7	14.2	14.0	51.1	51.1	50.8	50.8
Home equity holdings												
less than $50,000					34.1	34.2	33.0	33.2				
$50-90,000					48.7	48.9	43.0	43.2				
over $90,000					17.3	16.9	24.0	23.7				

a. 5+ rooms for renters; 7+ for owners.

TABLE 2.9 SELECTED HOUSING ATTRIBUTES BY AGE OF HEAD IN 2010 UNDER DIFFERENT ASSUMPTIONS (percentages)

	65-74				75-84				85+			
	Case (1)	Case (2)	Case (3)	Case (4)	Case (1)	Case (2)	Case (3)	Case (4)	Case (1)	Case (2)	Case (3)	Case (4)
Large unit (1=yes)[a]	19.7	18.8	31.8	31.0	11.4	10.7	17.4	16.7	12.7	12.2	17.3	16.1
Number of units in structure												
1	77.7	77.4	77.7	77.4	70.8	70.5	70.8	70.5	67.4	66.8	67.4	66.8
2-4	9.4	9.4	9.4	9.4	9.4	9.4	9.4	9.4	10.1	10.3	10.1	10.3
5-9	3.6	3.7	3.6	3.7	4.0	4.0	4.0	4.0	5.1	5.3	5.1	5.3
10+	9.4	9.5	9.4	9.5	15.8	16.0	15.8	16.0	17.4	17.6	17.4	17.6
Unit has structural deficiency	10.1	10.1	9.1	9.1	13.5	13.4	11.9	11.8	14.8	15.0	12.6	12.6
Unit has maintenance deficiency	2.3	2.3	2.5	2.5	2.1	2.0	2.9	2.8	2.9	3.0	3.5	3.6
Household spends over 30% of income on housing (1=yes)	19.0	18.8	19.4	19.3	24.3	24.3	24.4	24.4	33.9	33.8	33.6	33.5
Home equity holdings												
less than $50,000	31.1	31.2	29.5	29.6	36.5	36.5	35.9	36.0	36.7	37.0	36.5	36.8
$50-90,000	51.0	51.3	43.5	43.6	47.0	47.2	43.0	43.1	45.7	45.7	40.8	41.2
over $90,000	17.9	17.6	27.1	26.8	16.5	16.3	21.2	20.9	17.7	17.3	22.7	22.0

a. 5+ rooms for renters; 7+ rooms for owners.

TABLE 2.10 SELECTED HOUSING ATTRIBUTES BY HOUSEHOLD TYPE IN 2010 UNDER DIFFERENT ASSUMPTIONS (percentages)

	Husband-Wife Only				Husband-Wife w/others				Female Alone			
	Case (1)	Case (2)	Case (3)	Case (4)	Case (1)	Case (2)	Case (3)	Case (4)	Case (1)	Case (2)	Case (3)	Case (4)
Large unit (1=yes)[a]	16.2	16.1	34.7	34.5	63.4	62.9	65.7	65.4	5.7	5.7	6.6	6.6
Number of units in structure												
1	84.5	84.4	84.5	84.4	89.7	89.7	89.7	89.7	61.4	61.4	61.4	61.4
2-4	6.8	6.8	6.8	6.8	7.5	7.5	7.5	7.5	12.5	12.5	12.5	12.5
5-9	1.8	1.8	1.8	1.8	.9	.9	.9	.9	5.8	5.8	5.8	5.8
10+	6.9	7.0	6.9	7.0	1.9	1.9	1.9	1.9	20.4	20.4	20.4	20.4
Unit has structural deficiency	6.5	6.4	5.9	5.9	9.1	9.1	7.9	7.9	16.5	16.5	14.5	14.5
Unit has maintenance deficiency	.8	.8	.8	.8	2.0	1.8	2.0	1.8	2.8	2.8	3.9	3.9
Household spends over 30% of income on housing (1=yes)	4.7	4.6	5.0	5.0	7.1	7.1	7.4	7.4	44.7	44.7	44.7	44.7
Home equity holdings												
less than $50,000	22.4	22.5	21.0	21.0	20.6	20.7	19.6	19.8	50.7	50.7	50.5	50.5
$50-90,000	55.4	55.3	44.3	44.3	42.2	42.2	42.0	41.8	42.8	42.8	42.2	42.2
over $90,000	22.2	22.3	34.8	34.7	37.2	37.1	38.4	28.4	6.5	6.5	7.3	7.3

a. 5+ rooms for renters; 7+ rooms for owners.

	Male Alone				Other			
	Case (1)	Case (2)	Case (3)	Case (4)	Case (1)	Case (2)	Case (3)	Case (4)
Large unit (1=yes)[a]	5.5	5.5	7.2	7.2	37.0	36.7	45.1	44.6
Number of units in structure								
1	62.8	62.7	62.7	62.7	79.2	79.2	79.2	79.2
2-4	9.7	9.8	9.7	9.8	9.7	9.7	9.7	9.7
5-9	7.0	7.0	7.0	7.0	3.4	3.4	3.4	3.4
10+	20.5	20.5	20.5	20.5	7.7	7.7	77	7.7
Unit has structural deficiency	18.2	18.2	15.1	15.1	13.7	13.5	13.0	12.7
Unit has maintenance deficiency	3.7	3.7	4.4	4.4	5.5	5.5	5.4	5.4
Household spends over 30% of income on housing (1=yes)	16.7	16.7	16.7	16.7	30.1	30.2	30.6	30.6
Home equity holdings								
less than $50,000	41.8	41.8	41.8	41.8	38.5	38.8	35.7	36.0
$50-90,000	48.8	48.8	48.0	47.6	38.4	38.2	35.2	34.9
over $90,000	9.4	9.3	10.6	10.5	23.1'	23.0	29.2	29.2

a. 5+ rooms for renters; 7+ rooms for owners.

TABLE 2.11 SELECTED HOUSING ATTRIBUTES BY INCOME QUARTILE IN 2010 UNDER DIFFERENT ASSUMPTIONS (percentages)

	Lowest Quartile				2nd Quartile				3rd Quartile				Highest Quartile			
	Case (1)	Case (2)	Case (3)	Case (4)	Case (1)	Case (2)	Case (3)	Case (4)	Case (1)	Case (2)	Case (3)	Case (4)	Case (1)	Case (2)	Case (3)	Case (4)
Large unit (1=yes)[a]	5.4	5.3	5.4	5.3	4.7	4.6	6.5	6.2	6.2	5.7	13.6	13.2	44.2	42.6	69.2	68.1
Number of units in structure																
1	61.3	61.2	61.3	61.2	73.1	72.8	73.1	72.8	77.6	77.3	77.6	77.3	81.6	81.4	81.6	81.4
2-4	11.8	11.8	11.8	11.8	9.9	9.8	9.9	9.8	8.8	8.9	8.8	8.9	7.4	7.4	7.4	7.4
5-9	6.7	6.8	6.7	6.8	3.7	3.7	3.7	3.7	3.0	3.0	3.0	3.0	2.4	2.4	2.4	2.4
10+	20.2	20.2	20.2	20.2	13.3	13.7	13.3	13.7	10.7	10.8	10.7	10.8	8.6	8.8	8.6	8.8
Unit has structural deficiency	3.4	39.1	35.1	34.8	5.4	5.1	4.8	4.5	3.1	2.8	2.7	2.4	1.4	1.3	1.0	.9
Unit has maintenance deficiency	8.3	8.1	10.4	10.2	.4	.3	.4	.3	.3	.2	.3	.2	.2	.1	.2	.1
Household spends over 30% of income on housing (1=yes)	49.8	49.6	49.5	49.4	27.1	26.7	27.1	26.7	11.8	11.3	12.0	11.5	3.6	3.3	4.3	4.0
Home equity holdings	78.0	77.9	77.8	77.7	48.9	48.3	48.3	47.9	25.3	24.6	24.1	23.5	2.9	2.9	1.2	1.1
less than $50,000	20.6	20.7	20.7	20.8	48.9	49.5	48.8	49.2	67.6	68.3	62.9	63.4	48.7	48.8	34.1	34.0
$50-90,000	1.4	1.5	1.4	1.5	2.2	2.2	30.0	3.0	7.1	7.1	13.0	13.1	48.4	48.3	64.8	65.0
over $90,000																

a. 5+ rooms for renters; 7+ rooms for owners.

concentrate on the differences between cases 1 and 3 in our discussion.

The most obvious observation is that altering the assumptions about living arrangements makes much less difference than altering preferences about housing. This is due largely to the fact that, overall, the shifts in living arrangements are not large. In general, the altering of housing preferences from the base case results in bigger dwellings being occupied, somewhat greater equity holdings in the home, a decrease in structural deficiencies, and an increase in maintenance problems. Altered preferences have little effect on the type of unit occupied (e.g., single-family vs. multi-family), or on the share of income devoted to housing.

The incidence of elderly households living in large units increases substantially between the base case and the case in which the elderly of 2010 adopt the housing preferences of the next-younger generation. For all elderly, the incidence of occupying a large dwelling (i.e., 5+ rooms for renters, 7+ rooms for owners) rises from 15.2 to 23.8 percent. However, the entire increase results from homeowners living in larger units; their incidence rises from 14.4 to 25.8 percent, while there is actually a slight decline in the share of renters living in large units (table 2.8). Among the elderly of different ages, those in households headed by a person under age 75 in 2010 exhibit larger increases in the occupancy of large units than do older households (table 2.9). The increase for these younger households is large indeed, from 19.7 to 31.8 percent. This pattern mirrors that of younger nonelderly homeowners presently occupying larger units.

Two other groups of households would also experience very large increases in occupying larger units if housing preferences shifted in this way: husband-wife households and the highest income households. For these two groups, the increase in the percentage occupying large units increases from 16.2 to 34.7 and from 44.2 to 69.2 percent, respectively (tables 2.10 and 2.11). Thus, it is changes in the housing preferences of high-income homeowning couples among the younger elderly that drives the overall increase in occupancy of large units.

A similar pattern is evident, though less dramatic, for the increase in the value of home equity holdings. The clearest results are for husband-wife only households and those in the highest income quartile. For married couples, the increase in the percentage of households with equity holdings of over $90,000 is from 22.2 to 34.8 percent; for households in the highest income quartile, the increase is from 48.4 to 64.8 percent. In contrast, for those households in the lowest two income quartiles, who in some ways can benefit most from being able to draw down their home equity, there is little or no change in their equity holdings.

The impact of shifting preferences on the incidence of occupancy of dwellings with structural and maintenance deficiencies is more complex. In particular, the pattern is for the incidence of structural deficiencies to fall and for the incidence of maintenance deficiencies to rise. Across all households, both changes are small but definitely present. For structural problems the incidence falls from 12.1 to 10.7 percent; for maintenance problems the incidence rises from 2.3 to 2.8 percent. As noted earlier, these patterns are consistent with trends apparent for these two types of deficiencies since 1974. We believe that the improvement in structural quality is attributable to the overall improvement in the quality of the housing stock, which in turn is related to income growth and the share of income spent on housing. On the other hand, the rise in maintenance problems seems to be more associated with the characteristics of the elderly, and may well result from the financial and physical difficulties older homeowners have in performing dwelling maintenance.

With respect to the decline in the presence of structural deficiencies, there are some clear beneficiaries, heavily concentrated among renters. Households headed by a person aged 85 or over are one group of beneficiaries; their incidence falls from 14.8 to 12.6 percent. Likewise, persons living alone do well.[20] The biggest reduction, however, is for households in the lowest income quartile, whose incidence of occupancy of units with structural problems falls from 39.4 to 35.1 percent.

The groups that benefit with respect to structural defects are the same that lose with respect to maintenance defects, except it is homeowners, not renters, who are experiencing the problems. (Indeed, renters in general experience a slight decline in the incidence of maintenance problems.) The largest increase in the incidence of maintenance problems under the changed housing preferences simulation is experienced by those in the two oldest age categories--those living alone, and those in the lowest income quartile. Among these, the largest absolute increase is for those in the lowest income group, for whom the incidence rises from 8.3 to 10.4 percent.

The results of simulating the future housing circumstances of the elderly in 2010 under alternative assumptions about future developments offer two different but equally important kinds of results. First, they indicate that the results for the base case are quite robust, in that the general pattern of results is not highly sensitive to modest changes in two of the assumptions underlying them. The results of the base case are particularly robust with respect to the changes in living arrangements simulated.

Second, some thought-provoking results were obtained from simulating the future housing situation of the elderly under the assumption that their housing preferences change between now and the year 2010 from the present pattern to that of households in the next younger generation. Occupancy of larger units by younger, affluent, elderly homeowning couples was one definite pattern. With this shift comes the accumulation of greater housing wealth by the same households. Another important result is the reduction in structural deficiencies in rental units, especially units occupied by the oldest and poorest households and by persons living alone. Finally, an increase in maintenance defects among owner-occupied housing is evident--particularly for the oldest and poorest homeowners, and homeowners living alone.

We find the general situation depicted by the simulations embodying the changed housing preferences of the elderly to be more plausible than the base case. Although the alternative simulations may overstate the amount of adjustment in housing consumption that may take place, we believe that they are more realistic than the base case, which almost certainly understates the adjustment. For this reason, we use the data base for case 3 for our analysis of the impact of alternative federal government policy interventions on the future housing circumstances of the elderly presented in the next four chapters.

Notes, chapter two

1. After 2010, as the baby boomers reach retirement age, the young-elderly group grows rapidly.

2. TRIM2 computes income in 2010 prices. In deflating incomes back to 1984 prices, we used the simple CPI deflator.

3. We have excluded renters who occupy units without paying cash rent on the grounds that their very special housing circumstances do not make them of general interest. In 1978, such households were 3 percent of all elderly. Table B-1 presents some tabulations for this group in comparison with other elderly households.

4. As noted earlier 1978 was the year with the detailed data on activity limitations available. Given the very low mobility rates of the elderly (see Schneider, Stahl and Struyk, 1985; Newman and Reschovsky, 1987), their housing situation is unlikely to have changed much in the intervening period.

5. This finding is at odds with some other projections which indicate that mobile homes will grow in importance among the elderly. Tabulations prepared by Pitkin and Masnick (1980) reported in Struyk (1982).

6. There is a somewhat different pattern in the results for occupancy of a unit in a tall (4+ floors) structure. There is little overall change, actually a slight decline; and the highest income households increase their rate of occupancy of tall buildings even though their occupancy of large multifamily units declines. Thus, it appears that these households are favoring luxury high-rise projects.

7. Even households in the highest income quartiles are shown to have some households receiving assistance. The question asked on the CPS is very general and it is likely that households living in projects sponsored under the original Section 202 program, which were designed for moderate income households, are those appearing in this group. Also, those responding to the question may be participating in state or local programs for moderate income households.

8. A recent study estimated that about 2.0 million elderly households were receiving assistance in 1985, based on program data. For this reason, and because little growth in the number of households assisted by the traditional housing programs is in prospect, the number shown for 2010 is probably roughly correct. Struyk (1985), table 3.

9. The size of the task is increased by the fact that the subsidy contracts on a large number--well over one million--assisted housing units will expire in the years ahead, and Congress will have to appropriate more funds just to keep a constant number of assisted units.

10. The results are somewhat sensitive to the cutoff chosen. A much broader pattern of increase was evident when a five-or-more-rooms standards was used for all households.

11. For more information on this point, see Struyk (1982).

12. Manton (1980), Manton and Soldo (1985), Palmore (1976), Palmore (1986), Rice and Feldman (1983), Verbrugge (1984

13. For more on this pattern for the present day elderly, see Newman (1985).

14. See the first two rows of figures in table 2.6A.

15. The predictive functions used for the ratio of home equity to house value were not as useful as most of the other functions estimated because the Survey of Residential Finance used in this estimation only included a limited number of demographic variables. The ultimate result is that the estimated functions are capable of

predicting only a small number of different values, leading to considerable "bunching" in the predictions of equity amounts.

16. We considered several other adjustments which were not included in the final simulations (see appendix B for details).

17. See U.S. Bureau of the Census (1986).

18. By doing this, rather than defining all elderly to have the preferences of, say, 55 year olds, we have been able to preserve more variance in the incidence of the predicted attributes across the elderly. More details of this procedure are provided in appendix A.

19. The widespread use of home equity line loans is one factor that could alter this, but it is very hard to predict how widespread the use of this lending facility will be.

20. For females the decline is from 16.5 to 14.5 percent, while for males it is from 18.2 to 15.1 percent.

Chapter Three

IMPACTS OF AN EXPANDED HOUSING ALLOWANCE PROGRAM FOR RENTERS

As noted, the major housing assistance programs under which the low-income elderly are currently being added in substantial numbers are limited housing allowance-type programs. One obvious way of increasing such housing assistance is to expand the existing programs for renters. This chapter examines the potential impact of a sharply expanded housing allowance program for renters--one in which any income-eligible elderly household could participate--on the housing situation of the elderly in 2010. It provides estimates of the number of households likely to participate in such a program as well as the program's cost under several policy alternatives. It also shows how the program might affect, among other things, the incidence of housing deficiencies and excessive housing expenditures.

In FY 1987 the U.S. Department of Housing and Urban Development (HUD), which currently operates the housing voucher program for renters, budgeted enough funds to support approximately 49,000 vouchers--about half of all additional units funded that year under the voucher and Section 8 Existing programs together. Because of growing interest in the voucher concept, we chose to simulate a voucher program instead of the Section 8 Existing program, although simulation of an expansion of the Section 8 Existing program would yield similar conclusions.

If existing policies were continued unchanged, the share of elderly households residing in subsidized units would rise from about 21 percent in 1978 to around 31 percent in 2010 (see chapter 2). This increased participation is taken as a given in the simulations reported here. The estimates of the additional households assisted under an expanded renter voucher program exclude those households already receiving housing assistance in 2010 according to the simulations.

HUD's voucher program is closely related to its well-known Section 8 Existing housing subsidy program--a program in which participants find their own housing and the federal government pays a portion of the rent. Under the Section 8 program, an eligible household may rent a unit meeting minimum size and quality standards for an amount less than or equal to a predetermined rent level known as the Fair Market Rent (FMR). The federal government pays the difference between what a household can afford to pay (approximately 30 percent of adjusted gross income) and the applicable FMR. FMRs vary from place to place and are published in the Federal Register at least annually. They typically correspond to the 45th percentile of the rent distribution of standard quality rental housing, and are intended to be high enough so that households can find housing meeting program requirements.

Although the eligibility rules are basically the same for the two programs, HUD's voucher program differs from the Section 8 Existing program in several key areas.[1] Under the Section 8 program, a household spends 30 percent of its adjusted gross income regardless of what its landlord receives (an amount less than or equal to the applicable FMR). Under the voucher program, payment to a household is calculated using a "housing-gap formula," in which the subsidy payment is equal to the FMR minus 30 percent of adjusted gross income. A household is free to spend more than 30 percent of its adjusted gross income if it wants to consume more housing or less if it chooses to keep the residual rent savings for other purposes.

Housing quality standards are identical in the two programs. Such standards are an important component of housing allowance programs, because they ensure that participants will occupy housing that meets minimum health and safety criteria. Because a household not already living in an acceptable unit must either have its existing unit upgraded to meet these standards or move to an acceptable unit, quality standards affect the share of eligible households who will participate in the program.

SIMULATING A VOUCHER PROGRAM

This section explains how a simple computer model was developed to determine eligibility, calculate payments, and estimate participation for an open enrollment voucher program.

Determining Household Eligibility

The computer model developed for this analysis examined each household on the input file to determine whether or not it was eligible under the current regulations for HUD's rental voucher program, based upon its demographic characteristics and income. Elderly families and individuals living alone are eligible. In addition, in certain cases, a live-in helper is allowed to live in a qualifying nonfamily household when the head or spouse is handicapped or disabled.[2]

The model determined income eligibility by comparing a household's adjusted annual income to a cutoff point.[3] Income cutoff points vary according to location and household size, and are based on a value corresponding to 50 percent of the median income of four-person families. A household with an annual income falling below the applicable limit was income eligible for the program.[4]

Calculating Voucher Payments

Voucher payments were calculated using a housing-gap formula for those households that met the demographic and income requirements of the program. Under this housing-gap formula, a household's subsidy is equivalent to the FMR less the household's contribution, which is assumed to be 30 percent of its adjusted income.[5]

In order to select the proper FMR for a household, the number of bedrooms required by each household had to be determined. The model checked the size and composition of a household, and then assigned that household a certificate for a unit with an appropriate number of bedrooms. Only a very small percentage of elderly renter households require more than 2 bedrooms; most require only one. Computed subsidies were not allowed to exceed the FMR.

The model also calculated Public Housing Authority (PHA) administrative costs of the voucher program. These costs in 1987 consisted of a $215 preliminary (start-up) fee and an on-going fee of 6.5 percent of the 2-bedroom FMR. These fees are somewhat lower than those associated with the Section 8 Existing program.

Participation in a Voucher Program

Not every household eligible for the voucher program will end up participating in it. A number of steps must be successfully completed before an eligible household becomes a recipient. First, an eligible household must become aware of the program and enroll in it. Once enrolled, a household must then find a unit that meets minimum housing quality standards--and has the appropriate number of bedrooms for the household's composition. If the unit already occupied by a household does not meet these requirements, the household must either move to an acceptable unit or upgrade its present unit. These requirements ensure that safe, decent housing is occupied by participants, but they also discourage participation in the program for those not initially able to meet the requirements by raising the cost of obtaining acceptable housing.

The participation rates used in the model were derived from rates obtained from the Housing Assistance Supply Experiment (HASE).[6] In this experiment, an entitlement housing voucher program was conducted in Green Bay,

TABLE 3.1 PERCENTAGE OF ELIGIBLE RENTER HOUSEHOLDS BECOMING HOUSING ALLOWANCE RECIPIENTS IN THE SUPPLY EXPERIMENT UNDER THE 50% OF AREA MEDIAN INCOME ELIGIBILITY RULE

SOUTH BEND	Participation Rate	GREEN BAY	Participation Rate
Elderly couples	31	Elderly couples	40
Elderly individuals	51	Elderly individuals	78
All households	53	All households	60

Source: Zais, Struyk, Thibodeau (1982; p. 97).

Wisconsin, and South Bend, Indiana, over a period of 10 years. Table 3.1 displays the participation rates for elderly couples and individuals at both sites. The average of these rates was used. Thus, it was assumed that 65 percent of eligible elderly individuals and 36 percent of eligible elderly couples would participate. The rate for couples was applied to all eligible households with two or more persons. Households were randomly selected to be participants based on these rates.[7]

SIMULATION RESULTS

The rest of this chapter presents the results of simulating three different housing voucher programs for elderly renters:

- an entitlement program open to all eligible households,
- a program targeted on eligible households that spend excessive amounts of their income (more than 30 percent) on housing, and
- a program targeted on eligible households that occupy units with structural or maintenance deficiencies.

TABLE 3.2 SELECTED HOUSING ATTRIBUTES OF ALL ELDERLY RENTERS AND ELIGIBLE RENTERS IN 2010 (percentages)

	Renters	Eligible Renters
Large unit[a]	17.4	19.0
Number of units in structure		
1	18.9	27.6
2-4	22.0	26.1
5-9	13.6	14.3
10+	45.5	32.0
Unit has structural deficiency[b]	8.0	15.3
Unit has maintenance deficiency[b]	3.5	7.2
Household spends over 30% of income on housing	50.8	88.0

Source: Tabulations of augmented TRIM file.

a. 5 or more rooms.
b. HUD/Simonson definition.

As a starting point, it is helpful to describe how elderly renter households that are eligible for the voucher program (i.e., the entitlement version) will differ from elderly renter households in general in 2010 (table 3.2). Relative to all elderly renters, households eligible for the program tend to occupy structures with fewer units--especially single-family homes. This is consistent with the slightly higher tendency for this group to live in large units. The incidence of both structural and maintenance deficiencies among the eligible group is roughly twice that of all renters. As expected, the share of eligible households spending over 30 percent of income on housing, at 88 percent, exceeds that of all households. The share of all households spending excessive amounts, however, is still large at nearly 51 percent. Approximately 2.5 million elderly households are eligible to participate in a voucher program.

Program Costs and Participation

Table 3.3 displays cost and participation figures for the three versions of the program. The participation estimates range from 1.5 million households under the entitlement program to a mere 200,000 households in the program targeted on households occupying deficient units. It is noteworthy that participation and costs of the version targeted on households with excessive housing expenditures are similar to the entitlement version open to all eligible households. This reflects *the large share* of all low-income elderly households that spend more than 30 percent of gross income on housing.

Annual outlays for a voucher program consist of the yearly subsidy payments to households and the administrative fees paid to the PHAs which operate the program. The average annual payment is a little under $2,000 per recipient household (1984 dollars) for all three programs. The average for the program targeted on households with excessive expenditures is slightly higher than the others, primarily because households eligible for this program have incomes that are lower than the average for all eligible households. The on-going PHA administrative fees represent almost an eighth of annual outlays in the entitlement program. Together, annual subsidy payments and administrative fees amount to $3.3 billion for a program open to all eligible households. An additional $320 million is required for a one-time "start-up" fee to PHAs. In comparison, total current (FY1987) federal housing payments are about $9.5 billion (HUD 1987, H-21).

TABLE 3.3 PARTICIPATION AND COSTS UNDER THREE ALTERNATIVE VOUCHER PROGRAMS IN 2010 (1984 dollars)

	Program Open to All Eligible Households	Program Targeted on Eligible Households Spending More than 30% of Income on Housing	Program Targeted on Eligible Households Living in Deficient Units
Participants (millions)	1.5	1.3	0.2
Average subsidy per participant ($)	1,899	1,991	1,952
Annual Cost ($ billions)			
Subsidy	2.86	2.66	0.47
On-going PHA fee	0.44	0.40	0.06
Start-up PHA fee	0.32	0.29	0.05

Impact on Housing Conditions

In simulating the impact of the program on housing conditions, two key assumptions were made. It was assumed that participants would occupy units free of structural and maintenance defects. In addition, it was assumed that households spending over 30 percent of income on housing before participating in the program no longer spent that much after becoming recipients[8]. To simplify the presentation, figures are presented for the entitlement version of the program only. Note that the success of the other more sharply targeted programs in eliminating particular problems is largely a function of the participation rates for those programs, since all the households eligible for those programs have at least one problem, and all the participants will eliminate these problems according to the assumptions just stated. We

TABLE 3.4 SELECTED HOUSING ATTRIBUTES OF ELIGIBLE RENTERS BEFORE AND AFTER IMPLEMENTATION OF AN EXPANDED VOUCHER PROGRAM IN 2010 (percentages)

	Before	After
Unit has structural deficiency[a]	15.3	6.7
Unit has maintenance deficiency[a]	7.2	3.4
Household spends over 30% of income on housing	88.0	34.5
Receives housing assistance	0.0[b]	60.1

a. HUD/Simonson definition.
b. Only households not receiving subsidies are eligible for the program.

focus on several key variables that are directly affected by the voucher program: the incidence of structural and maintenance deficiencies, the share of households with excessive housing expenditures, and the percentage of units subsidized by the program. The latter figure is equivalent to the participation rate.

The program has a significant impact on housing conditions among the eligible population (table 3.4). Both structural and maintenance deficiencies would be cut by more than half. In addition, the share of households spending more than 30 percent of their income on housing would fall dramatically, from 88 to 35 percent. This is largely attributable to the fact that three-fifths of all eligible households are expected to participate.

Households in the lowest income quartile would have the greatest decreases in defects and rent burden (table 3.5). Households in the first quartile, which initially possess by far the highest rate of deficiencies and incidence of excessive expenditures, would have the highest participation rate--nearly 65 percent, and there would be a big drop in rent burden for households in all quartiles, especially for those in the poorest one. Importantly, close to 95 percent of

TABLE 3.5 SELECTED HOUSING ATTRIBUTES OF ELIGIBLE RENTERS BEFORE AND AFTER IMPLEMENTATION, BY INCOME QUARTILE[a] (percentages)

	Lowest Quartile		2nd Quartile		3rd Quartile	
	Before	After	Before	After	Before	After
Unit has structural deficiency[b]	23.9	10.4	6.5	3.0	0.6	0.0
Unit has maintenance deficiency[b]	11.8	5.0	2.3	1.7	1.3	0.8
Household spends over 30% of income on housing	93.2	32.8	83.9	37.1	69.9	30.0
Receives housing assistance	--	64.7	--	55.5	--	51.7

a. Percent distribution of eligible households by income quartile: first quartile 52.2%; second quartile 42.4%; third quartile 5.4%. No households in the highest quartile would be eligible for the program.
b. HUD/Simonson definition.

TABLE 3.6 SELECTED HOUSING ATTRIBUTES OF ELIGIBLE RENTERS[a] BEFORE AND AFTER PROGRAM IMPLEMENTATION, BY AGE (percentages)

	65-74		75-84		85+	
	Before	After	Before	After	Before	After
Unit has structural deficiency[b]	18.7	8.9	11.7	4.7	17.8	7.1
Unit has maintenance deficiency[b]	9.4	4.3	5.3	2.6	7.7	3.1
Household spends over 30% of income on housing	84.3	37.1	89.9	34.3	91.2	29.0
Receives housing assistance	--	54.5	--	61.9	--	68.4

a. Percent distribution of eligible households by age: 65-74 years 37.8%; 75-84 years 46.6%; 85+ years 15.6%.
b. HUD/Simonson definition.

TABLE 3.7 SELECTED HOUSING ATTRIBUTES OF ELIGIBLE RENTERS BEFORE AND AFTER PROGRAM IMPLEMENTATION, BY HOUSEHOLD COMPOSITION[a] (percentages)

	Husband-wife Only		Husband-wife w/Others		Female Alone		Male Alone		Others	
	Before	After	Before	After	Before	After	Before	After	Before	After
Unit has structural deficiency[b]	18.3	11.0	28.9	21.4	10.4	3.4	24.6	10.1	19.1	12.4
Unit has maintenance deficiency[b]	9.4	6.4	15.4	13.2	4.2	1.3	10.4	3.6	16.2	11.2
Household spends over 30% of income on housing	63.7	37.4	57.3	28.2	99.6	32.1	71.4	30.2	93.8	61.7
Receives housing assistance	--	41.8	--	45.7	--	67.8	--	61.2	--	32.9

a. Percent distribution of eligible households by income quartile:

Husband-wife only	13.4%
Husband-wife with others	1.4
Female alone	57.4
Male alone	20.6

b. HUD/Simonson definition.

all eligible households are projected to be in the two lowest quartiles.

There are smaller variations by age (table 3.6). A higher share of older elderly households would participate than the younger elderly; this is because they tend to have lower incomes. The incidence of deficiencies would drop by about half for all groups. Households in the oldest age group, those headed by a person 85 years of age or older, would have the greatest drop in rent burden--91 to 29 percent. However, it should be noted that only about 16 percent of eligible renters fall into this age group; nearly half of the eligible households are headed by persons between the ages of 75 and 84.

With respect to household composition (table 3.7) the most dramatic finding is that the incidence of excessive expenditures among females living alone, which would be especially high if current policies continued, would be reduced by over two thirds.

Notes, chapter three

1. For a detailed comparison of the two programs, see Kennedy and Finkel (1987).

2. According to Current Population Survey data, in 1985 roughly 98 percent of all elderly-headed households were comprised of families or single persons (Bureau of the Census, 1985). Thus, there are few non-family households. As a simplification with respect to household composition requirements, the model allowed any type of elderly-headed household to be eligible with the exception of those categorized as living in group quarters, which is defined here as any unit with five or more persons.

3. Household income includes wages or salaries, self-employment income, Social Security, railroad retirement, Supplemental Security Income, Aid to Families with Dependent Children, other public assistance, interest, dividends, income from estates or trusts, rental income, veterans payments, unemployment compensation, workmen's compensation, private pensions, government pensions, alimony or child support, and regular contributions from persons

not living in the dwelling unit. When a household has net family assets exceeding $5,000, federal regulations require that the income figure used to determine eligibility include either the income from these assets or a percentage of the value of these assets (equivalent to the passbook savings rate), whichever is greater. Because asset value (other than home equity for homeowners) was not present on the data set, an asset value was imputed for renters by summing interest, dividend, royalty, estate, trust, and rental income and assuming that this income represented a 5.5 percent return on asset value. After a household's income was adjusted to reflect asset holdings, it was then compared to the maximum income limit for program participants.

4. The median income of a four-person household, which is used to determine income eligibility limits, is expected to increase around 40 percent in real terms between 1984 and 2010. An implicit assumption made in our analysis is that housing expenditures will rise in real terms along with incomes. But as real incomes increase, poor households--as defined by an absolute measure of well-being such as the poverty line--are going to become a smaller share of the population. HUD may have to revise its income eligibility guidelines by the year 2010. A lower eligibility limit could dramatically lower participation and costs.

5. Adjusted income was calculated by subtracting deductions for minors and elderly households from gross income. A $480 deduction was permitted for each household member under 18 years of age other than the head or spouse. All households in the data set qualified for a $400 deduction that is granted to elderly households. Although the regulations permit additional deductions for child care and medical expenses under certain conditions, the model did not incorporate these allowances. For the purpose of calculating payments, the definition of gross income included income from assets--the income definition using the percent-of-assets rule was used only to determine income eligibility.

6. Lowry (1983) and Struyk and Bendick (1981) contain excellent reviews of the Supply Experiment.

7. On the one hand, the rates may be high because HASE did an excellent job in notifying eligible households about the program. On the other hand, there is reason to believe these rates may be lower than the participation rates which would apply in a program

implemented today. Evidence from the current housing voucher demonstration (Kennedy and Finkel 1987) indicates that a significant increase in the rate at which enrollees are successful in becoming participants in the Section 8 Existing Program occurred between 1979 and 1987. However, these results apply to a limited entitlement program, so it is not clear that they are applicable to a full entitlement program. Taking all of this information together, the participation rates in the table seem reasonable.

8. The results of HASE and the ongoing voucher experiment both show that a sizable share of participants in voucher programs (over 40 percent) spend more than 30 percent of their income on housing. Nevertheless, we continue to use the rule just cited in the text for two reasons. First, if the FMRs are set correctly, the household could rent a unit at or below the FMR and thus spend no more than 30 percent of its income. Spending more is its choice. Second, we are simulating the results for a generic housing allowance program. If the Section 8 program is continued rather than the voucher program, the rule would hold by definition.

Chapter Four

HOUSING ALLOWANCES FOR HOMEOWNERS

Homeowners have not been eligible to participate in housing allowance programs in the United States. The emphasis in homeownership assistance is on helping households become homeowners. Such aid is provided through large subsidies embodied in the federal income tax provisions, the large program of loan interest rate write-downs administered by the Farmers Home Administration (Section 502), the subsidies embodied in the low interest rate mortgages supported by tax exempt Mortgage Revenue Bonds offered by state and local governments, and the residual assistance program (Section 235) operated by the Department of Housing and Urban Development. One factor in the policy to exclude homeowners from voucher eligibility may be that most elderly homeowners have been able to receive assistance through these various mechanisms. This is not a good reason to exclude them from additional assistance later in life, however, since no one has suggested that renter households who obtained housing assistance earlier in life, and who remain income eligible for assistance as older persons, should not continue to receive it. Another factor may be the perception that elderly homeowners do not need subsidization because of the equity they have built up in their homes. There is no question that home equity has been the principal form of wealth accumulation in this country. However, there are ways to take home equity holdings into account in determining eligibility for payments and payment levels on an equitable basis, as discussed below. Indeed, such procedures were shown to be administratively feasible in the Housing Allowance Supply Experiment (Lowry 1983).

SIMULATING A HOMEOWNER VOUCHER PROGRAM

The basic simulation methodology employed is the same as for the expanded rental voucher program. The rules for participating in the voucher program for homeowners are assumed to be the same as for renters. Real property holdings in the form of home equity play a greater role in determining eligibility for homeowners than for renters, however. Recall that for the purpose of determining eligibility, income includes 5.5 percent of the value of equity in real property. Thus, households can report low amounts of income from sources such as wages and salaries or social security, yet still be ineligible for the program because of large real property holdings. Since a large share of elderly homeowners are free from mortgage debt, this source of "income" can have a significant impact on voucher eligibility for homeowners.

One of the key differences between the programs for renters and homeowners lies in the anticipated participation rates. Evidence from the Housing Assistance Supply Experiment (HASE) suggests that homeowners would participate at a lower rate than renters. We assumed that, under the 50 percent of median income eligibility rule, 65 percent of single-person households and 36 percent of other households would participate in the rental voucher program. We do not have information on the participation of elderly homeowners under the 50 percent of median income eligibility rule from the Supply Experiment, but we do have participation rates for elderly homeowners under an eligibility guideline roughly corresponding to 80 percent of median income. To approximate homeowner participation rates under the 50 percent rule, we used the ratio between the homeowner and renter participation rates under the "80 percent" eligibility rule to adjust downward the rates we previously used for renters. Observing that elderly renters participated at rates that were about 55 percent greater than those of elderly homeowners in the Supply Experiment, we estimated that 42 percent of eligible single-person homeowner households and 23 percent of other eligible households would participate.[1]

There are several reasons why it is plausible to expect homeowners to participate at lower rates than renters. As noted previously, to participate in the voucher program, a household's dwelling unit must meet minimum standards. If a household's home does not meet these requirements, the household must either upgrade it or move to an acceptable unit. To move, a homeowner may have to take on a new mortgage or become a renter. Both of these options may be undesirable, especially for an elderly homeowner. In the Supply Experiment, both homeowners and renters receiving payments were more likely to have upgraded their units than they were to have moved to meet housing quality standards.[2]

SIMULATION RESULTS

Table 4.1 compares some housing attributes of elderly homeowners eligible to participate in a housing voucher program with all elderly homeowners as of 2010. Both groups are similar with respect to the number of units in the structures occupied by households. The dominant type of unit is the single-family home. The units occupied by eligible households, however, tend to be smaller than average; only 2.9 percent of eligible owners occupy large units, whereas 25.8 percent of all owners have large units. The share of units with maintenance deficiencies among the eligible owner population is slightly more than double than that of all owners. The same is true for structural deficiencies although the share of units in this category is only about a quarter of that of maintenance deficiencies. Eligible owners also have lower home equity holdings than owners in general. This reflects the lower incomes of eligible households as well as the effect of home equity holdings on income eligibility.[3] Not surprisingly, the share of eligible homeowners spending over 30 percent of their income on housing--at 27 percent--is roughly twice that of all owners.

TABLE 4.1 SELECTED HOUSING ATTRIBUTES OF ALL ELDERLY HOMEOWNERS AND ELIGIBLE HOMEOWNERS IN 2010 (percentages)

	All Homeowners	Eligible Homeowners
Large unit[a]	25.8	2.9
Number of units in structure		
1	91.0	92.0
2-4	5.4	5.7
5-9	0.8	0.5
10+	2.7	1.9
Unit has structural deficiency[b]	11.6	25.6
Unit has maintenance deficiency[b]	2.5	6.1
Household spends over 30% of income on housing	14.2	27.0
Home equity holdings[c]		
Under $50,000	33.0	64.0
$50,000 - 89,999	43.0	33.6
$90,000 or more	24.0	2.4

Source: Tabulations of augmented TRIM file.
a. 7 or more rooms.
b. Same definition as used in earlier chapters (HUD/Simonson).
c. In 1984 dollars. Figures for all homeowners exclude mobile homes; figures for eligible homeowners include mobile homes.

Participation and Costs

Just as we did for renters, we simulated three different voucher programs including:

- an entitlement program open to all eligible homeowners,
- a program targeted on eligible homeowner households that spend more than 30 percent of their income on housing, and

- a program targeted on eligible homeowner households that occupy units with structural or maintenance deficiencies.

Table 4.2 displays estimated participation and costs under the three programs.

In an entitlement program open to all eligible households, approximately 2.8 million households are projected to participate out of an eligible population of around 7.8 million households. The programs targeted on households with excessive housing expenditures and dwelling deficiencies are fairly similar with respect to size and cost. Each of these programs is projected to have roughly one-fourth as many participants as the entitlement program, because a large share of those eligible for the entitlement version do not have one of the traditional housing problems. The average subsidy per participant in each of the more sharply targeted programs is projected to be higher than for the entitlement version due to the tendency for households with these particular housing problems to have lower incomes.

The projected participation and costs of the homeowner voucher program differ from the expanded rental voucher program in several interesting respects. Although the average annual subsidy per participant is similar among the targeted nonentitlement programs, the average subsidy for the homeowner entitlement program is $300 less than that of the renter entitlement program. As a result, even though the number of households participating in the homeowner entitlement program is nearly twice that participating in the renter entitlement program, the annual cost at $5.2 billion (including subsidy payments and the ongoing PHA fee) is only about one-and-a-half times as large.

The entitlement version of the homeowner voucher program is much larger and more expensive than either the excess cost burden or deficiency versions. Both nonentitlement versions are projected to be quite small, with each serving around 700,000 households. Because there is likely to be some overlap between households who qualify for

TABLE 4.2 PARTICIPATION AND COSTS UNDER THREE ALTERNATIVE HOMEOWNER VOUCHER PROGRAMS IN 2010 (1984 dollars)

	Program Targeted on All Eligible Households	Program Targeted on Eligible Households Spending More than 30% of Income on Housing	Program Targeted on Eligible Households Living in Deficient Units
Participants (millions of households)	2.8	0.8	0.7
Average subsidy per participant ($)	1,598	2,113	1,864
Annual Cost ($ billions)			
Subsidy	4.41	1.73	1.37
On-going PHA fee	0.75	0.24	0.18
Start-up PHA fee	0.59	0.18	0.16

these programs, the two programs might be combined into a single program targeted on households with excessive housing expenditures and/or dwelling deficiencies that would cost only about half what an entitlement program would cost.

Impact on Housing Conditions

The remainder of this discussion, which deals with the impact of the homeowner voucher program on housing conditions, focuses on the entitlement version of the program only. Like the renter versions of these programs, the success of the more sharply targeted programs in eliminating particular problems is largely a function of the participation rates for those programs, since all the households eligible for those programs have at least one problem, and all the participants will eliminate these problems according to our assumptions.

Table 4.3 shows the overall impact that an entitlement voucher program might have on the eligible homeowner population. The share of units with structural deficiencies would drop by around 37 percent; the share of units with maintenance deficiencies would drop by roughly 46 percent--from 6.1 to 3.3 percent of income eligible homeowners. The incidence of households spending over 30 percent of income on housing would decline about 39 percent--from 27.0 to 16.4 percent.

In general, the homeowner voucher program is projected to have smaller impacts on the housing situation of the elderly than a similar renter program. An important factor leading to these lower estimated effects is our assumption that the overall participation rate of homeowners would be much lower than that of renters.

A breakdown of the housing circumstances of eligible households by income quartile before and after implementation of the voucher program for homeowners is presented in table 4.4. Maintenance deficiencies, which are projected to exist only among households in the lowest income quartile, are projected to be cut nearly in half, to an incidence rate of 7.3 percent of the eligible households in this income class.[4] As in the renter program, the highest participation rates are found among households in the two poorest quartiles, which together account for nearly 97 percent of all eligible households. The poorest quartile--which is projected to have the highest rate of deficiencies and incidence of excessive housing expenditures in the absence of the new program--is also estimated to have the greatest improvement. Only a modest improvement is seen for households in the third quartile, which in any case has only 3.4 percent of eligible households.

There are few differences among the various indicators with respect to age. This is partly due to similar participation rates projected for the different age groups. The share of households with any given problem drops to 50 to 65 percent of its size in the absence of the program. One group does stand out somewhat: a relatively high share of households in the oldest age category (head 85 years of age

TABLE 4.3 SELECTED HOUSING ATTRIBUTES OF ELIGIBLE HOMEOWNERS BEFORE AND AFTER IMPLEMENTATION OF A VOUCHER PROGRAM IN 2010 (percentages)

	Before	After
Unit has structural deficiency[a]	25.6	16.1
Unit has maintenance deficiency[a]	6.1	3.3
Household spends over 30% of income on housing	27.0	16.4
Receives housing assistance	--	35.6

a. HUD/Simonson definition.

TABLE 4.4 SELECTED HOUSING ATTRIBUTES OF ELIGIBLE HOMEOWNERS BEFORE AND AFTER PROGRAM IMPLEMENTATION, BY INCOME QUARTILE[a] (percentages)

	Lowest Quartile		2nd Quartile		3rd Quartile	
	Before	After	Before	After	Before	After
Unit has structural deficiency[b]	50.7	31.3	4.9	3.6	8.6	6.1
Unit has maintenance deficiency[b]	13.6	7.3	0.0	0.0	0.0	0.0
Household spends over 30% of income on housing	38.3	22.5	17.5	11.2	20.9	16.2
Receives housing assistance	--	38.1	--	34.5	--	18.8

a. Percent distribution of eligible households by income quartile: first quartile 44.9%; second quartile 51.7%; third quartile 3.4%. No households in the highest quartile would be eligible for the program.
b. HUD/Simonson definition.

TABLE 4.5 SELECTED HOUSING ATTRIBUTES OF ELIGIBLE HOMEOWNERS BEFORE AND AFTER PROGRAM IMPLEMENTATION, BY HOUSEHOLD COMPOSITION[a] (percentages)

	Husband-wife Only		Husband-wife w/Others		Female Alone		Male Alone		Others	
	Before	After	Before	After	Before	After	Before	After	Before	After
Unit has structural deficiency[b]	16.8	11.9	28.1	19.4	24.9	17.2	28.8	17.3	28.6	24.2
Unit has maintenance deficiency[b]	2.0	1.1	7.1	5.5	7.8	3.7	7.2	4.2	9.8	7.9
Household spends over 30% of income on housing	4.2	3.4	19.1	15.6	45.1	25.5	2.2	1.2	39.5	32.2
Receives housing assistance	--	25.5	--	19.7	--	43.3	--	40.8	--	23.1

a. Percent distribution of eligible households by household composition:

Husband-wife only	30.3%
Husband-wife with others	2.5
Female alone	49.2
Male alone	10.8
Other	7.1

b. HUD/Simonson definition.

or more) spends over 30 percent of their income on housing both before and after implementation of the program (36 percent before; 22 percent after). This is largely attributable to the low incomes of this group. As in the renter program, the majority of eligible households--in this case 53 percent--are headed by a person 75 to 84 years of age.

Table 4.5 shows selected housing attributes of eligible households by household composition. Husband-wife homeowners make up a third of eligible households. The largest group--females living alone--accounts for half of the total. Males living alone and "other" households make up the remainder. With respect to deficiencies, husband-wife only households have the lowest incidence rates without and with the program. Female homeowners living alone are among the worst off in terms of deficiencies and housing expenses without the program, but are projected to make the greatest gains because their participation rate is the highest of any group. Relatively small shares of both husband-wife only households and males living alone spend excessive amounts on housing before and after program implementation.

Notes, chapter four

1. Struyk and Bendick (1981) Table 4.2.

2. See Struyk and Bendick (1981) pp. 99-100, 107-108. Mobility was an important means of meeting standards for those occupying housing with multiple deficiencies.

3. Other tabulations not presented here confirm that households with the lowest incomes have less equity on average and also show that younger elderly households tend to have accumulated less equity. This latter observation merely reflects the fact that younger elderly households are more likely than their older counterparts to still have mortgage debt on their homes.

4. Even in the renter version of the program, the incidence of maintenance deficiencies among eligible households in the second and third quartiles was quite small--less than 2.5 percent. It is

unlikely that no homeowner households in these quartiles have maintenance deficiencies. The observed pattern is probably the result of our imputation procedures that tended to exaggerate existing trends.

Chapter Five

THE EFFECTS OF AN INCREASE IN THE USE OF HOME EQUITY CONVERSION MORTGAGES[1]

We have seen that homeownership is the dominant tenure form among the elderly. For most elderly households the equity in their home represents the majority of their net worth,[2] and the vast majority of these homeowners have eliminated the mortgage debt on their homes. This equity is seldom drawn upon to support consumption, however, largely because it has been difficult to access without having to sell one's home. In the past few years, new financial instruments, known collectively as HECMs have been developed to permit the elderly to use their equity for current expenses while continuing to live in their homes. In this chapter we explore the income-generating potential of HECMs and estimate the effect of this additional income on the housing situation of elderly homeowners in the year 2010. We begin by describing several types of HECMs, including the type used in our simulation.

HOME EQUITY CONVERSION MORTGAGES

Although a wide variety of HECMs have been developed, a considerably smaller number are now actually being marketed. Here we review a few of the more prominent types.[3]

Fixed Debt Loans without Guaranteed Lifetime Tenure

Under these loans, debt increases (as monthly payments are made to the borrower) for a specified term, usually 5-10 years, at the end of which the loan is repayable. Under such a plan, the lender would loan up to 80 percent of the home's equity value at a market interest rate. This loan differs from a traditional home equity loan in that it does not require the borrower to make any periodic repayments. Total repayment is made at the end of the loan term. The principal disadvantage of this type of instrument, and the reason why it has not been attractive to borrowers, is that it must be paid off at the end of the term; hence, the borrower could be in the position of having neither a home nor assets at the end of the term, if the house has not appreciated enough to permit further borrowing.[4]

Fixed Debt Loans with Guaranteed Lifetime Tenure

These loans are designed to overcome the objection to the nonlifetime option just reviewed. Under this instrument, the borrower uses available home equity to borrow a lump sum from a lending institution; the institution requires that the proceeds be used to purchase a single premium immediate annuity from a life insurance company. As with all annuities, the amount of income generated would depend on the age of the borrower at the time of the purchase and on the borrower's sex, both of which are critical determinants of life expectancy. Out of this gross annuity, interest only is paid to the lender on the fixed debt. The remainder would be monthly income to the borrower which would continue for life. At the borrower's death, the debt is paid off, either by the estate or through sale of the house. The main limitation of this instrument is that should the homeowner die soon after the purchase of the annuity, she would receive little income and the debt would still have to be satisfied.[5]

Rising Debt Loans for Tax Deferral

One public plan that guarantees occupancy and provides some additional disposable income is a deferred tax payment plan. Under this arrangement, the state in effect makes a loan to a homeowner by allowing the homeowner to defer property tax payments. Interest is charged by the state (often at a below market rate) on the outstanding balance; the debt is satisfied at the time of death or sale of the unit from the proceeds of the sale. Because of the subsidy involved (through the low interest rate charged on the balance), some states have income tests for participation. California is one state offering such property tax payment deferrals, and participation has been fairly high. The chief limitation of this option is the small amount of income it generates for the borrower compared to other options.

Combination Loan-Equity Plans

None of the options reviewed thus far explicitly incorporate consideration of the increase in home equity that will accrue from appreciation in house values over the life of the loan contract. Loan-equity plans take advantage of this source of increased equity. They involve the borrower acquiring both a debt and the obligation to share with the the lender the possible appreciation. Instruments of this type are called shared appreciation mortgages.

The borrower receives monthly income payments based on below market interest rates, in exchange for which the investor obtains a share of the appreciation. The greater the lender's share of the appreciation, the greater the payments received by the borrower. Payments continue for life or until sale. At this point, the loan balance, including interest plus the share of appreciation, is due. Annuity income is related to life expectancy as well as to initial home value.[6]

Our calculations of the income potential of HECMs for the elderly employ one version of the shared appreciation mortgage. It is a plan being offered in 1987 through Prudential-Bache Mortgage Services in the Philadelphia metropolitan area and in the state of New Jersey. Under the "Century Plan," the borrower pledges a specific fraction of the home's future appreciation in exchange for a loan interest rate below current market rates. Borrowers receive fixed monthly payments for as long as they remain in their homes, with the amount based on their current home value and their age(s). The figures in table 5.1 give an idea of the monthly income borrowers of different ages could expect to receive on homes of $40,000 and $100,000, given interest charges on payments made to the borrower of 11.5 percent per year and all appreciation in the home being assigned to the lender. Clearly, payments rise with age.

Borrowers may pay off the loan at any time, with their liability limited to their accumulated principal and interest or 94 percent of the value of the home, whichever is lower. The general pattern of cost to the borrower depends on the interest rate on the loan, the amount of appreciation forgone, and the length of time payments are received. The overall pattern of costs is as follows: (a) short-term loans are very expensive; (b) when the loan term equals the borrower's life expectancy and the annual average appreciation is about 6 percent (and appreciation is fully assigned to the lender), then the combined interest rate is roughly equivalent to that charged by major credit card companies; and, (c) when the loan term exceeds the borrower's life expectancy and appreciation is less than 6 percent, the combined interest rate will likely be below market interest rates. Obviously, it is by pooling loans that the Century Plan is intended to internalize various forms of risk.[7,8]

SIMULATING AN INCREASE IN THE USE OF HECM

Using the same data set that we used earlier for simulating an expanded homeownership voucher program, we developed a simple computer model that identified eligible households, calculated HECM payments under the Century Plan, selected participants, and estimated the effect of higher incomes on the housing situation of participating homeowners.

TABLE 5.1 EXAMPLES OF MONTHLY PAYMENTS UNDER THE CENTURY PLAN[a] (dollars)

Age of Owner	Monthly Payment When Home Value is $40,000		Monthly Payment When Initial Home Value is $100,000	
	Single	Married	Single	Married
70	142	85	399	245
75	180	108	496	332
80	261	172	720	472
85	343	251	924	679

Source: American Homestead Corporation.

a. All appreciation accrues to lender. Fixed interest rate of 11.5%.

To be eligible for a HECM in our simulation, a household and its property had to meet several criteria. Eligibility was restricted to husband-wife only and single-person households in which the head or spouse was at least 75 years of age. In the case of couples, both persons had to be at least 70. Payments were based on the age of the youngest person in a household which could not exceed 85 years. Households occupying mobile homes, farms, and units which were not owned free and clear were ineligible. About 6.6 million households were eligible based on these criteria.

HECM payments were based on a schedule prepared by American Homestead which is summarized in table 5.1. This table shows the monthly payments for different combinations of home equity and borrower's age under the Century Plan. The payments are based on an 11.5 percent interest rate. We used a simple interpolation technique to derive equations that calculated payments for all age and home value combinations not in the table.

As discussed earlier, numerous factors such as life expectancy, payment size, and risk exposure are likely to affect participation in a HECM program. Given the low rate of acceptance of HECMs and the increasing use of home equity loans, which would to some degree substitute for HECMs, a low participation rate seems in order. We have arbitrarily assumed that 10 percent of eligible households would participate. We have restricted the selection of participants, however, to those households whose incomes would increase by at least 15 percent as the result of HECM payments. About 80 percent of eligible households have incomes that would increase this much; therefore, about 12.5 percent of these households are expected to participate under our simulation. We believe that this is a conservative estimate of participation.

SIMULATION RESULTS

In reviewing the results of this simulation it is important to remember two things. First, the number of households expected to participate is small--about 671,000 out of an eligible pool of around 6.6 million. Thus, from the outset we anticipate that the program would have fairly small impacts on the homeowner population eligible for HECMs. Second, the effects of the HECM program on housing conditions stem purely from increased income. There are no minimally acceptable standards of quality, unlike a housing voucher program. To the extent that households choose not to spend their increased income on housing, there will be no effect.

Characteristics of the Eligible Population

Eligible households are more likely than elderly homeowner households in general to occupy small units--a characteristic consistent with the somewhat greater tendency for this group to occupy units in multifamily structures (table 5.2). Eligible homeowners also tend to have lower incomes. This is further reflected in somewhat lower equity holdings, a

TABLE 5.2 SELECTED HOUSING ATTRIBUTES OF ALL ELDERLY HOMEOWNERS AND ELIGIBLE HOMEOWNERS IN 2010 (percentages)

	All Homeowners	Eligible Homeowners
Large unit[a]	25.8	13.4
Number of units in structure		
1	91.0	87.9
2-4	5.4	6.8
5-9	.8	0.9
10+	2.7	4.4
Unit has structural deficiency[b]	11.6	14.2
Unit has maintenance deficiency[b]	2.5	3.3
Household spends over 30% of income on housing	14.2	16.4
Unit has major dwelling modification[c]	2.2	2.0
Unit has minor dwelling modification[d]	7.3	8.8
Home equity holdings[e]		
Under $50,000	33.0	36.5
$50,000 - $89,999	43.0	44.8
$90,000 or more	24.0	18.7
Percent with no mortgage debt	91.7	100.0
Income Quartile		
Lowest	18.6	26.3
Second	24.9	29.7
Third	27.2	24.9
Highest	29.2	19.1

Source: Tabulations of augmented TRIM file.

a. 7 or more rooms.
b. HUD/Simonson definition.
c. Includes: ramps; elevator or stair lift; extra-wide doors; special sinks, faucets or cabinets; or bathroom designed for wheelchair use.
d. Includes extra handrails or grabbars; door handles instead of knobs; push bars on doors; special wall sockets or light switches; raised lettering or braille; specially equipped phone; or flashing lights.
e. In 1984 dollars.

TABLE 5.3 SELECTED HOUSING ATTRIBUTES OF ELIGIBLE HOMEOWNERS BEFORE AND AFTER AN INCREASE IN THE USE OF HECMs IN 2010 (percentages)

	Before	After
Unit has structural deficiency[a]	14.2	13.8
Unit has maintenance deficiency[a]	3.3	3.2
Household spends over 30% of income on housing	16.4	15.6
Unit has major dwelling modification[b]	2.0	2.2
Unit has minor dwelling modification[c]	8.8	9.3

a. HUD/Simonson definition.
b. Includes: ramps; elevator or stair lift; extra-wide doors; special sinks, faucets or cabinets; or bathroom designed for wheelchair use.
c. Includes extra handrails or grabbars; door handles instead of knobs; push bars on doors; special wall sockets or light switches; raised lettering or braille; specially equipped phone; or flashing lights.

higher incidence of deficiencies, and a slightly greater share of households spending more than 30 percent of their income on housing.

Impact on Housing Conditions

The overall impact of the increased use of HECMs is summarized in table 5.3. As expected, the effects on the eligible population are projected to be small: a slight reduction in structural and maintenance deficiencies and in the percentage of households spending excessive amounts of income on housing.[9] The increased income from HECMs will also stimulate only a small increase in the incidence of both major and minor dwelling modifications.

TABLE 5.4 SELECTED HOUSING ATTRIBUTES OF ELIGIBLE HOMEOWNERS BEFORE AND AFTER AN INCREASE IN THE USE OF HECMs IN 2010, BY INCOME QUARTILE[a]

	Lowest Quartile		2nd Quartile		3rd Quartile		Highest Quartile	
	Before	After	Before	After	Before	After	Before	After
Unit has structural deficiency[b]	50.1	48.3	2.1	2.1	1.2	1.2	0.7	0.7
Unit has maintenance deficiency[b]	12.5	12.1	0.0	0.0	0.0	0.0	0.0	0.0
Household spends over 30% of income on housing	40.6	39.7	15.2	13.9	3.6	3.2	1.5	1.4
Unit has major dwelling modification[c]	1.2	1.8	1.9	2.1	1.2	0.9	4.4	4.4
Unit has minor dwelling modification[d]	15.9	17.6	11.0	11.0	4.4	4.4	1.5	1.5

a. Percent distribution of eligible households by income qauartile:

First quartile	26.3%	Third quartile	24.9
Second quartile	29.7	Fourth Quartile	19.1

b. HUD/Simonson definition.

c. Includes: ramps; elevator or stair lift; extra-wide doors; special sinks, faucets or cabinets; or bathroom designed for wheelchair use.

d. Includes: extra handrails or grabbars; door handles instead of knobs; push bars on doors; special wall sockets or light switches; raised lettering or braille; specially equipped phone; or flashing lights.

TABLE 5.5 SELECTED HOUSING ATTRIBUTES OF ELIGIBLE HOMEOWNERS BEFORE AND AFTER AN INCREASE IN THE USE OF HECMs IN 2010, BY HOUSEHOLD TYPE[a]

	Husband-Wife Only		Female Alone		Male Alone	
	Before	After	Before	After	Before	After
Unit has structural deficiency[b]	7.3	7.1	20.2	19.4	18.4	17.6
Unit has maintenance deficiency[b]	1.1	1.1	5.2	5.0	4.5	4.4
Household spends over 30% of income on housing	0.0	0.0	36.2	34.6	0.0	0.0
Unit has major dwelling modification[c]	3.2	3.2	1.3	1.7	0.0	0.0
Unit has minor dwelling modification[d]	2.2	2.2	17.4	18.4	0.0	0.0

a. Percent distribution of eligible households by household composition:

Husband-wife only	44.6%
Female Alone	45.2
Male Alone	10.3

b. HUD/Simonson definition.

c. Includes: ramps; elevator or stair lift; extra-wide doors; special sinks, faucets or cabinets; or bathroom designed for wheelchair use.

d. Includes: extra handrails or grabbars; door handles instead of knobs; push bars on doors; special wall sockets or light switches; raised lettering or braille; specially equipped phone; or flashing lights.

Although the overall impact on the eligible population is small, some interesting patterns emerge when we examine the impact that the widespread availability of HECMs has on certain subgroups--in particular, low-income households and households consisting of females living alone.

The benefits of HECMs, for example, vary by income quartile (table 5.4). The decrease in dwelling deficiencies will be concentrated among households in the lowest income quartile--a group which initially had the highest incidence of deficiencies. Similarly, the increase in dwelling modifications is confined to the two lowest quartiles. The effect on excess cost burden will not differ much by income, however. The share of households spending more than 30 percent of their incomes on housing is projected to decrease slightly for each income quartile.

Females living alone will benefit more than proportionately from HECMs (table 5.5). The increases in dwelling modifications and the reductions in the share of households spending excessive amounts on housing, for example, are projected to occur solely among females living alone. All three types of household experience a lower incidence of structural deficiencies; all groups except husband-wife households are projected to have reduced maintenance deficiencies.

Like low-income households generally, females living alone are the primary beneficiaries of improved housing conditions resulting from the widespread availability of HECMs. However, even for this group, the impact of HECMs is not large: over a third of these households will still spend excessive amounts of their incomes on housing and nearly a fifth still occupy units with structural deficiencies (about 18 percent of males living alone also occupy structurally deficient units).

Notes, chapter 5

1. Parts of this chapter draw heavily from Struyk, Rice, and Keare (1987).

2. Friedman and Sjogren (1981).

3. This section draws heavily from Springer (1985).

4. Use of this type of loan was pioneered by the San Francisco Development Fund working with lenders in northern California.

5. There are also limited rising debt loans with guaranteed lifetime tenure. For an example, see Springer (1985), pp. 13-14.

6. A variant on this model has been offered by the city of Buffalo to its elderly homeowners under which the city takes care of maintenance and does rehabilitation needed at the time the contract is signed. For details, see Weinrobe (1985).

7. For more on the Century Plan, see Scholen et al. (1984).

8. Another type of HECM involves a sale-leaseback arrangement. In this case the borrower sells his home to a private investor; the investor then leases it back to the borrower. Although conceptually no rent need be paid, without such consideration the borrower and buyer may not be able to use certain tax advantages (such as depreciation deduction for the investor and the one-time capital gains exclusion for the borrower). The borrower continues to live in the house but surrenders all rights after death. One example of this type of arrangement is the Fouratt plan. This plan is described in Springer (1985), pp. 16-17.

9. The small impact of HECMs on housing expense burden can be partly accounted for by the size of the HECM payments. For more than half of the participants, the percentage increase in income is under 35 percent; over three quarters of them have income increases of less than 55 percent. To put this into perspective, a household spending 40 percent of its income on housing needs its income to increase by at least a third (assuming it does not spend more on housing) for it to spend less than 30 percent of its income on housing; a household spending 50 percent must have its income increase by at least two thirds to achieve the same result. The average monthly HECM payment for participants is $314 (1984 dollars).

Chapter Six

THE IMPACTS OF A CONGREGATE HOUSING VOUCHER PROGRAM

The cost of providing a satisfactory living environment for the chronically ill and frail elderly is of major concern to policymakers.[1] This population, which contains many individuals incapable of independent living, has traditionally been served by nursing homes or similar long-term care facilities. A key characteristic of these facilities is that they provide substantial medical support to residents. Some studies suggest, however, that as much as 12 to 60 percent of the elderly living in such facilities could reside in the community if they received appropriate, primarily nonmedical, supportive services.[2] Congregate housing can serve just such a function. By offering services such as meal plans, transportation, housekeeping, and recreation, congregate housing facilities can foster independent living by households who might otherwise enter institutions. Furthermore, congregate housing appears to be less expensive than long-term care facilities for comparable levels of service. Heumann, et al. (1985) conducted a careful analysis which suggests that congregate facilities are about one-third less expensive than long-term care facilities.

An important measure of success for a congregate housing program is the degree to which the program delays or prevents institutionalization. It has not been conclusively shown, however, that congregate housing affects institutionalization rates.[3] In recent years there has been some indication that the supply of residences in long-term care facilities has not kept up with demand; indeed, the federal government has tried to limit the growth in the number of beds in intermediate care facilities. Thus, the population we have projected for the year 2010, which consists strictly of the noninstitutionalized population, contains many households who would occupy nursing homes and other long-term care facilities if they were available to do so. Under these conditions, there is the potential for a high demand for congregate facilities.

We have simulated a congregate housing voucher program that would be targeted strictly on the frail elderly. The voucher would entitle the holder to occupy a unit in a congregate housing project that provides for independent living with nonmedical support services, and would help pay the cost of the housing and support services. Households would contribute 50 percent of their incomes toward the cost because some meals and other services are included in addition to housing services. Note that this percentage falls between the 30 percent of (adjusted) income that households pay toward their rent when they receive housing assistance and the 100 percent of income (except for the $25 and $50 per month for incidental expenses) that people pay when they are in an intermediate care facility and being assisted by Medicaid.

The congregate housing projects would be privately developed, financed, owned, and operated, and would be open to households who were either owners or renters at the time they applied. Vouchers could only be used in the projects--not at home--both to take advantage of economies of scale that result from service provision to many users at one location and to reduce the incentive to substitute government for family-provided help that may exist under more dispersed service provision arrangements. Projects would be encouraged to serve voucher holders as well as "market rate" households. Eligibility for vouchers would be restricted to persons who meet the income criteria for housing assistance and are judged to be at high risk of institutionalization.

SIMULATING A CONGREGATE HOUSING VOUCHER PROGRAM

The rules for participating in the program used by our model are straightforward. Any household with a head or spouse with activity limitations would be eligible to participate as long as the household was not already occupying a subsidized unit or did not live in group quarters. (Activity limitations were the only measure of incapacity available in the Aged TRIM2 file.) Income eligibility criteria would be the same as for the voucher program we simulated earlier. Households not income eligible for vouchers and households income eligible but not otherwise entitled to receive a subsidy could still reside in congregate housing units as market rate participants.

The cost of congregate housing units was determined by adding an amount that covers the expense of various congregate housing services to the appropriate FMR of a household. The cost of services was based on items included in Heumann's (1985) definition of intermediate congregate housing services which consists of a secure, barrier-free apartment, a full meal plan, a basic sundry item budget, self-administered laundry, specialized door-to-door transportation (e.g., vans or cabs), and occasional heavy housekeeping assistance.[4]

The annual cost of congregate housing services (excluding rent and utilities, which are covered by the FMR) is projected to be $1,536 (1984 dollars) for an individual living alone or the first person in a household, and $1,248 for each additional person in a household. The cost of additional persons is somewhat less than the first person in a household because we assumed that the marginal cost of housekeeping attributable to additional household members was negligible and therefore excluded a housekeeping charge for additional members. The per person cost of other congregate housing services is not likely to vary much with household size.

We assumed that 20 percent of the eligible households would participate in the program. This rate is somewhat lower than those used in the voucher program simulations presented earlier for two reasons. First, the fact that households must move to a congregate facility to participate would act as a disincentive. Second, the contribution rate for subsidy-eligible households at 50 percent is higher than the 30 percent rate of the regular voucher program; this acts as an additional disincentive. We also assumed that a market rate household whose housing expenditure (i.e., Fair Market Rent) would exceed 30 percent of its income if it participated would choose not to participate.[5] In addition, we assumed that a market rate household would occupy at least a two-bedroom unit; others would be assigned to different size units according to regular voucher program rules.

All participating households, by definition, become renters who occupy units that meet minimum physical standards (i.e., units free of structural and maintenance deficiencies) and feature both major and minor dwelling modifications. Also by definition, all participants spend less than 30 percent of their income on housing (i.e., avoid any excess cost burden)--the additional 20 percent contribution that a household makes being viewed as a contribution towards congregate housing expenses other than rent and utilities.

SIMULATION RESULTS

The congregate housing program simulated here is projected to be of modest size in terms of participation and cost (table 6.1). Of the approximately 650,000 participating households, about 70 percent would receive subsidies. The number of subsidized participants, at under half a million, is less than a third of the size of the entitlement version of the rental voucher program that we simulated earlier. In

TABLE 6.1 PARTICIPATION AND ANNUAL COSTS UNDER A CONGREGATE HOUSING PROGRAM IN 2010 (1984 dollars)

	Subsidized	Market Rate
Participants (number)	465,211	185,531
Average subsidy per participant	2,319	--
Average housing subsidy per participant	1,542	--
Annual Cost (billions)		
Subsidy	1.1	--
On-going PHA fee	0.1	--
Start-up PHA fee	0.1	--

addition, despite a larger household contribution, the average annual subsidy under the congregate housing program is larger--$2,319 versus $1,899. On average, however, two thirds of the subsidy for a congregate housing program participant is made up of a "housing subsidy," which is the payment a household would receive if it participated in a "regular" voucher program. The average housing subsidy of subsidized congregate housing program participants is about four fifths the size of the average subsidy received by participants in the entitlement version of our simulated rental voucher program. The $1.2 billion annual cost of the congregate housing program is slightly more than one-third of the rental entitlement program cost.

Characteristics of Eligible Households

There are clear differences between the housing characteristics of households eligible to reside in congregate housing units (including market rate households) and all elderly-headed households (table 6.2). Eligible households

TABLE 6.2 SELECTED HOUSING ATTRIBUTES OF ALL ELDERLY HOUSEHOLDS AND HOUSEHOLDS ELIGIBLE FOR A CONGREGATE HOUSING PROGRAM IN 2010 (percentages)

	All Households	Eligible Households
Unit has structural deficiency[a]	10.7	20.0
Unit has maintenance deficiency[a]	2.8	6.9
Household spends over 30% of income on housing	23.1	40.3
Unit has major dwelling modification[b]	3.0	17.1
Unit has minor dwelling modification[c]	7.4	45.2
Large unit[d]	23.8	14.9
Number of units in structure		
1	73.5	78.5
2-4	9.4	9.7
5-9	3.9	2.3
10+	13.1	9.4

a. HUD/Simonson definition.

b. Includes: ramps; elevator or stair lift; extra-wide doors; special sinks, faucets or cabinets; or bathroom designed for wheelchair use.

c. Includes: extra handrails or grabbars; door handles instead of knobs; push bars on doors; special wall sockets or light switches; raised lettering or braille; specially equipped phone; or flashing lights.

d. 5 or more rooms for renters; 7 or more rooms for homeowners.

occupy units with structural and maintenance deficiencies and pay more than 30 percent of their incomes on housing at rates that are roughly double those of all elderly households. A hefty 40 percent of eligible households pay excessive amounts for housing.

These high rates largely reflect the fact that incomes are relatively low for this group--a group made up almost entirely of households with heads 75 years of age or older. (Recall that all eligible households have heads or spouses with activity limitations--a characteristic associated with increased age.) There also is a tendency for eligible households to occupy single-family homes and smaller units; only 15 percent of eligible households reside in large units, whereas 24 percent of all elderly households occupy such units. The incidence of both major and minor dwelling modifications among eligible households is about six times greater than the incidence of these modifications among all elderly households. This is consistent with our expectation that dwelling modifications are more likely to be found in units occupied by households that have members with activity limitations.

Impact on Housing Conditions

The overall impact that the program has on the eligible population is summarized in table 6.3. The rates at which households occupy units with structural and maintenance deficiencies and spend over 30 percent of their incomes on housing each drop to around 75 to 80 percent of their size before the program. The greatest absolute drop occurs in the share of households spending over 30 percent of their incomes on housing, which falls from 40 percent to 32 percent.

One of the more dramatic changes resulting from the program is the increased incidence of dwelling modifications. The share of households with major dwelling modifications doubles, to 34 percent, while the share with minor dwelling modifications increases by nearly a third, to 59 percent. The

TABLE 6.3 SELECTED HOUSING ATTRIBUTES OF ELIGIBLE HOUSEHOLDS BEFORE AND AFTER IMPLEMENTATION OF A CONGREGATE HOUSING PROGRAM IN 2010 (percentages)

	Before	After
Unit has structural deficiency[a]	20.1	16.1
Unit has maintenance deficiency[a]	6.9	5.2
Household spends over 30% of income on housing	40.3	32.3
Unit has major dwelling modification[b]	17.1	34.4
Unit has minor dwelling modification[c]	45.2	58.6

a. HUD/Simonson definition.
b. Includes: ramps; elevator or stair lift; extra-wide doors; special sinks, faucets or cabinets; or bathroom designed for wheelchair use.
c. Includes: extra handrails or grabbars; door handles instead of knobs; push bars on doors; special wall sockets or light switches; raised lettering or braille; specially equipped phone; or flashing lights.

incidence of minor dwelling modifications does not increase as much as that of major dwelling modifications, because a large share of households already had such modifications before they moved to congregate facilities. In this situation, there is a high probability that the minor dwelling modifications of a congregate facility will simply serve as a substitute for similar features of the housing previously occupied by participants.

The differential impacts of a congregate housing program by household type are shown in table 6.4. The vast majority (86 percent) of the eligible population consists of individuals and husband-wife couples. Females living alone make up

TABLE 6.4 SELECTED HOUSING ATTRIBUTES OF ELIGIBLE HOUSEHOLDS BEFORE AND AFTER IMPLEMENTATION OF A CONGREGATE HOUSING PROGRAM, BY HOUSEHOLD COMPOSITION[a] (percentages)

	Husband-wife Only		Husband-wife w/Others		Female Alone		Male Alone		Others	
	Before	After	Before	After	Before	After	Before	After	Before	After
Unit has structural deficiency[b]	13.1	8.2	10.6	2.9	23.6	20.2	22.9	19.5	21.9	18.4
Unit has maintenance deficiency[b]	2.6	1.5	6.3	2.9	8.7	6.4	12.6	12.6	8.3	7.4
Household spends over 30% of income on housing	3.7	2.1	2.8	2.8	62.1	49.3	24.3	20.9	43.2	37.9
Unit has major dwelling modification[c]	18.8	39.6	36.4	66.2	11.2	27.8	15.6	18.9	37.0	49.3
Unit has minor dwelling modification[d]	10.7	34.2	24.4	55.9	55.1	65.5	72.4	75.8	83.5	84.6

a. Percent distribution of eligible households by household composition:

Husband-wife only	29.5%	Male alone	2.8
Husband-wife with others	2.1	Other	11.8
Female alone	53.8		

b. HUD/Simonson definition.

c. Includes: ramps; elevator or stair lift; extra-wide doors; special sinks, faucets or cabinets; or bathroom designed for wheelchair use.

d. Includes: extra handrails or grabbars; door handles instead of knobs; push bars on doors; special wall sockets or light switches; raised lettering or braille; specially equipped phone; or flashing lights.

around 54 percent of all eligible households. This latter group has the biggest absolute drop in the share of households spending more than 30 percent of their incomes on housing--nearly 13 percent--but close to half of this group still spends excessive amounts on housing after the program is implemented. In addition, this group, along with husband-wife households (including households comprised of husband-wife couples with others) have the sharpest increases in major and minor dwelling modificiations.

About 71 percent of the eligible households have incomes falling below the median value for all elderly-headed households. Table 6.5 shows that while households in all quartiles benefit, households in the lowest quartile show the greatest improvements with respect to reductions in deficiencies and spending excessive amounts of income on housing. However, as in the other programs we have simulated, the incidence of these problems remains relatively high for the poorest quartile even after the program is implemented.

With the exception of major dwelling modifications for households in the highest income quartile, households in all quartiles have comparable absolute percentage increases in dwelling modifications--around 17 to 20 percentage points for major dwelling modifications and about 13 percentage points for minor dwelling modifications. However, the incidence of dwelling modifications, especially major modifications, is initially much higher for the households with the highest incomes. This is consistent with our expectation that wealthy households possess the resources to live in well-equipped housing. As a corollary, all else equal, we would expect to find lower-income households occupying such housing less frequently. Indeed, this overall pattern can be observed in table 6.5.

Notes, chapter 6

1. Parts of this chapter draw heavily from Struyk, Turner, and Ueno (1988).

TABLE 6.5 SELECTED HOUSING ATTRIBUTES OF ELIGIBLE HOUSEHOLDS BEFORE AND AFTER IMPLEMENTATION OF A CONGREGATE HOUSING PROGRAM, BY INCOME QUARTILE[a] (percentages)

	Lowest Quartile		2nd Quartile		3rd Quartile		Highest Quartile	
	Before	After	Before	After	Before	After	Before	After
Unit has structural deficiency[b]	43.4	35.7	6.0	4.2	4.4	3.0	1.0	0.2
Unit has maintenance deficiency[b]	17.1	12.8	0.2	0.2	0.1	0.0	0.0	0.0
Household spends over 30% of income on housing	62.8	50.0	34.9	28.4	19.0	16.2	9.6	5.7
Unit has major dwelling modification[c]	5.2	22.5	15.0	35.0	15.3	32.6	70.6	79.5
Unit has minor dwelling modification[d]	41.3	54.8	49.3	62.8	40.1	53.4	56.5	69.2

a. Percent distribution of eligible households by income qauartile:

First quartile	39.7%	Third quartile	18.4
Second quartile	31.1	Fourth Quartile	10.8

b. HUD/Simonson definition.

c. Includes: ramps; elevator or stair lift; extra-wide doors; special sinks, faucets or cabinets; or bathroom designed for wheelchair use.

d. Includes: extra handrails or grabbars; door handles instead of knobs; push bars on doors; special wall sockets or light switches; raised lettering or braille; specially equipped phone; or flashing lights.

2. See Heumann et al. (1985).

3. An evaluation of the Congregate Housing Services Program (CHSP) discovered that by the end of the demonstration period there was no significant difference in the rate at which participants and controls were permanently placed in institutions, but there was a difference in the rate at which the two groups were temporarily institutionalized over the period: 15 percent of experimentals versus 23 percent of controls (Sherwood, et al., 1985, Table IV.2). Still, analysts need to consider several problems with the demonstration and its evaluation in reaching a balanced judgment about congregate housing. Particularly important are the following: (a) the population served by the program was not restricted to people who were vulnerable to institutionalization; (b) the CHSP was structured around the provision of twice-a-day meals, a service that many of the participants neither needed nor especially wanted; (c) many of the control projects offered fairly rich service environments themselves, minimizing the possibility of finding an effect; (d) the observation period may have been too short, given the kind of program and control projects employed in the demonstration. Even with all the problems just listed some significant effects may have been evident over another year or two.

4. We adjusted Heumann's figures by substituting the FMR for rent and utilities, and reducing the cost of a meal plan by two thirds to approximate the cost of a one meal per day service. Cost figures, as elsewhere in this report, have been converted to 1984 dollars.

5. Establishing a participation rate is tricky because changes in the eligible base population can result from the program. To the extent that the program does prevent institutionalization, the size of the noninstitutionalized eligible population increases. However, as noted in the text, the noninstitutionalized population that we have projected for the year 2010 already contains many households who would occupy nursing homes and other long-term care facilities if they were available. Thus, institutionalization is already being delayed for many households, and congregate housing is likely to serve as a substitute for the existing homes of some of these households. As a result, we do not anticipate that the size of the noninstitutionalized population would change appreciably because of the congregate housing program proposed here, assuming that past trends in the supply of long-term care facilities persist.

Chapter Seven

SUMMARY AND COMPARISON OF THE INITIATIVES

If there are no changes in housing policy for the elderly between now and 2010, 2.7 million of the units in which elderly households live will have a structural deficiency, 0.7 million will have a maintenance deficiency, and 5.8 million elderly households will bear an excess cost burden. The analysis reported in previous chapters has explored the impacts on the housing problems faced by the elderly of four policy alternatives:

- an expanded housing voucher program for low-income elderly renters,
- a housing voucher program for low-income elderly homeowners,
- increased use of Home Equity Conversion Mortgage, and
- a congregate housing voucher for low-income impaired elderly.

As we proceed to summarize and compare these initiatives it is important to be aware that the populations they serve are quite different and that we should therefore not expect similar results. The renter voucher program, for example, naturally tends to serve the poorest households. Thus, it is not surprising that the greatest reduction in the share of households spending excessive amounts on housing was found in this program--a program with an eligible population possessing especially low incomes and not enjoying the economic benefits of owning a home free and clear as many elderly homeowners do.

In general, each of the initiatives analyzed serves a somewhat different population--in terms of income, tenure, and other initial housing circumstances--and each has somewhat different impacts on the three aspects of housing studied here: occupancy of a suitable unit by an impaired person, occupancy of a deficient unit, and devoting an extraordinary share of income to housing. Policymakers considering the use (or the expanded use in the case of rental vouchers and HECMs) of one of these programs, need to keep in mind the characteristics of the populations to be assisted.

IMPACTS ON THE HOUSING OF ELIGIBLE HOUSEHOLDS

The previous chapters discussed program effects in terms of the proportional impacts on the population of households eligible for a program. From this perspective, expanded housing vouchers for renters are projected to be the most effective. Housing vouchers for homeowners have the next greatest impact. Projected expansion in the use of HECMs would have very little impact on any of the three types of housing problems, in large part because households are not required to meet any minimum standards for the dwelling unit. Congregate housing vouchers have impacts that are greater than those of HECMs but smaller than those of the other low-income voucher programs.

The simulations point out that the greatest reductions in housing expense burden and improvements in housing quality stem from enforced housing quality standards and earmarked subsidies in government sponsored housing programs. HECMs can substantially raise incomes, but do not cause improvements in housing conditions the way voucher programs do. HECMs, however, do not require subsidies, whereas vouchers involve large government outlays.

Expanded Housing Vouchers for Renters

An expanded housing voucher program for renters is projected to have substantial impacts on housing conditions for the eligible population (see figure 7.1). The entitlement version of the program, for example, will cut both structural and maintenance deficiencies of eligible households in half, with the greatest benefit going to women and men living alone. Husband-wife families are projected to have a relatively high incidence of deficiencies before and after the program, in part because of low participation rates.

The proportion of households paying an excess burden will be cut by more than half, with the greatest benefits going to women living alone. The share of the poorest quarter of households spending excess amounts on housing is expected to drop from 93 percent to 33 percent. Importantly, close to 95 percent of all eligible households will have below-average incomes. Households in the 85 years or older group will also have a large drop in excess cost burden (91 to 29 percent), but only about 16 percent of renters in 2010 will fall into this group.

Housing Vouchers for Homeowners

The impacts of a voucher program for homeowners on housing conditions of the eligible population will be proportionately more modest than the impacts of an expanded program for renters, because of a lower overall participation rate (see figure 7.2). The proportion of eligible households in units with structural deficiencies will drop by 37 percent (from 25.6 to 16.1 percent). The proportion in units with maintenance deficiencies will drop by 46 percent (from 6.1 to 3.3 percent). The proportion with an excess cost burden will drop by 39 percent (from 27 to 16 percent).

FIGURE 7.1
IMPACT OF EXPANDED HOUSING PROGRAM FOR RENTERS ON HOUSING PROBLEMS OF ELIGIBLES

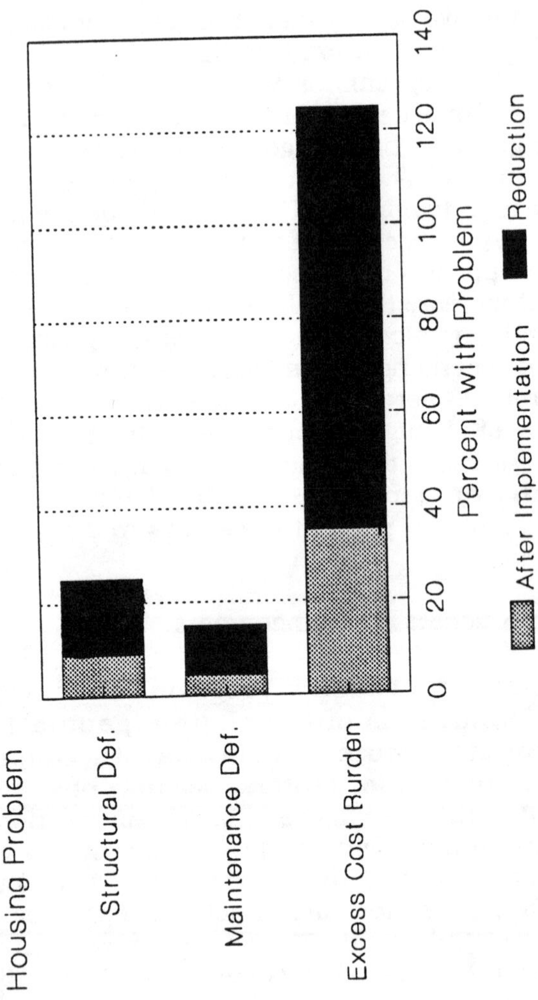

2.5 M. eligibles, 1.5 M. participants.
Estimated by The Urban Institute

FIGURE 7.2
IMPACT OF HOUSING VOUCHER PROGRAM FOR HOMEOWNERS ON PROBLEMS OF ELIGIBLES

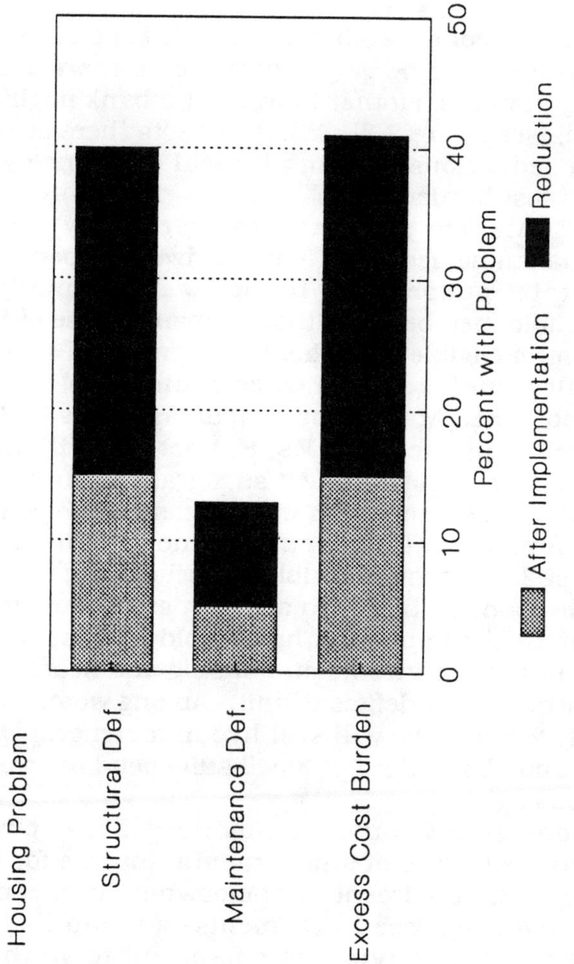

7.8 M. eligibles, 2.8 M participants.
Estimated by The Urban Institute

Elderly women living alone are among the worst-off before the program in terms of both structural deficiencies and excess cost burden (though not maintenance deficiencies); they also make the greatest gains.

Expanded Use of Home Equity Conversion Mortgages (HECMs)

The impacts of expanded use of HECMs on housing quality are projected to be very minor, since there are no formal quality standards (other than what a bank might require for a loan) (see figure 7.3). What impacts there are encompass minor reductions in both physical deficiencies and in the excess cost burden.

HECMs are projected to be equally ineffective in stimulating homeowners to make dwelling modifications that facilitate independent living by functionally impaired household members. Without expanded use of HECMs, 2.0 percent of eligible households are projected to have a major modification (such as a wheelchair ramp) in their home; expanded HECM availability increases this to 2.2 percent. Without expanded HECMs, 8.8 percent will have a minor dwelling modification (such as a grab bar in the bathroom); with them this proportion will increase to 9.3 percent.

Changes that do occur are mostly found among the poorest 25 percent of eligible households and among women who live alone. But even after program implementation, 4 out of 10 of the poorest households will spend an excess amount of their income on housing and nearly half will live in a structurally deficient unit. Among women living alone, nearly 2 out of 10 will still live in a structurally deficient unit, and about 1 out of 3 will still spend an excess amount on housing.

Home equity conversion mortgages may prove to be an important source of supplemental income for the elderly. But even if 10 percent of homeowners between 75 and 85 years old use these instruments--a group that will obtain large monthly payments compared to younger elderly

FIGURE 7.3
IMPACT OF INCREASE USE OF RAMs ON
HOUSING PROBLEMS OF ELIGIBLE HOUSEHOLDS

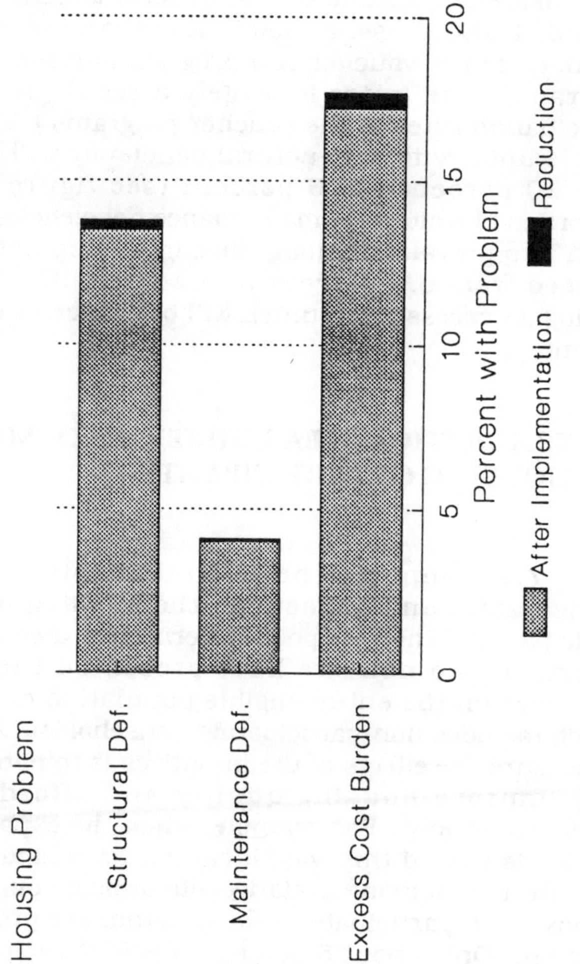

6.6 M. eligibles, 0.66 M. participants
Estimated by The Urban Institute

homeowners--the impact on the housing quality of this population will be small.

Congregate Housing Vouchers

The effects on quality and affordability of housing for households eligible under the congregate housing voucher program are projected to be considerably larger than those of expanded HECM use, although less than the effects of an expanded renter voucher or a program homeowner voucher program. (The latter is largely a result of the higher participation rates in the voucher programs.) The share of eligible units with a structural deficiency will be reduced from 20 percent to 16 percent (see figure 7.4). The proportion of units with maintenance deficiencies, which are much less prevalent among the eligible population, will be reduced from 6.9 percent to 5.2 percent. Households bearing an excess cost burden will be reduced from 40 to 32 percent.

COSTS, POLITICAL FEASIBILITY, AND IMPACTS ON THE HOUSING OF PARTICIPANTS

Table 7.1 compares the annual subsidy, number of participants, and impacts on the housing problems of participants of the four policy alternatives discussed in this report. Up to now, we have presented the impact of initiatives on the entire eligible population of households (which includes non-participating households). Another way to measure the effects of the initiatives is to note how much they improve housing quality and affordability for participants only. For example, when the expanded use of HECMs is viewed this way, it cannot be considered to be a very effective housing initiative--its impacts on the housing of those who participate in the program are projected to be minimal. Only about 5 percent of HECM recipients would

FIGURE 7.4
IMPACT OF CONGREGATE HOUSING VOUCHER PROGRAM ON HOUSING PROBLEMS OF ELIGIBLES

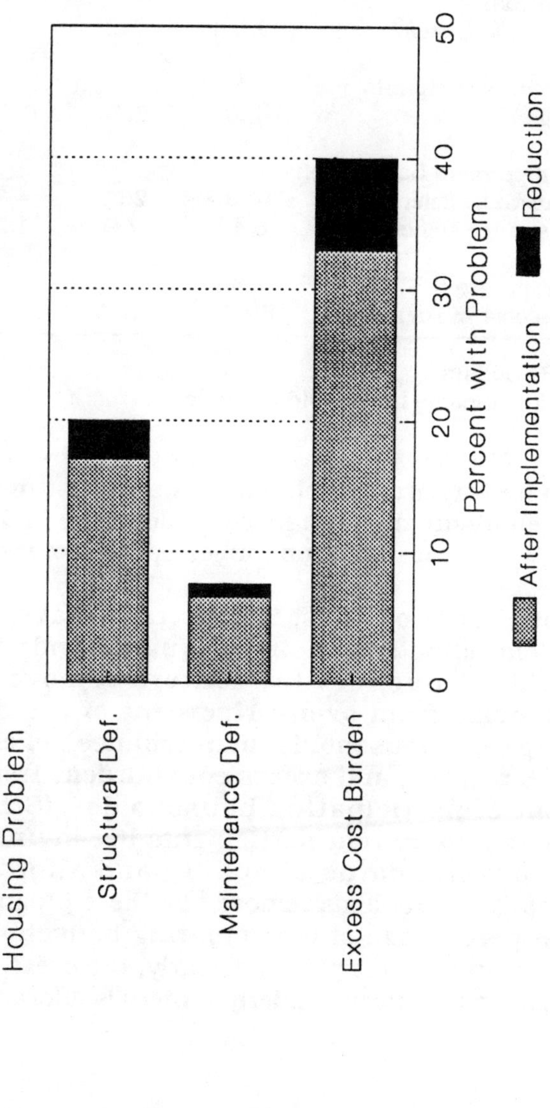

3.25 M. eligibles, 0.65 M. participants
Estimated by The Urban Institute

TABLE 7.1 IMPACTS ON HOUSING OF PARTICIPANTS AND COSTS OF DIFFERENT POLICY OPTIONS IN 2010

	Rental Voucher[b]	Owner Voucher[b]	RAM	Congregate Voucher
Total Annual Subsidy ($billions)[a]	3.3	5.2	--	1.2
Number of participants (millions)	1.50	2.76	0.67	0.65
Housing problem because of:				
Structural Deficiency	14.3	26.7	4.8	18.7
Maintenance Deficiency	6.4	7.9	1.2	8.2
Without program				
Excess cost burden	89.0	29.6	7.3	38.2

a. 1984 dollars.
b. All low-income households eligible.

eliminate structural deficiencies and just over 1 percent would eliminate maintenance deficiencies. In addition, only about 7 percent would no longer spend excessive amounts on housing.

Voucher programs, in contrast, have substantial beneficial effects on housing quality and affordability. Expanded vouchers for renters remove structural deficiencies from over 14 percent of the dwellings of participating households, maintenance deficiencies from about 6 percent, and excess cost burdens from almost 90 percent of participating households. (Since housing vouchers require that participants live in units that meet minimum standards of quality and affordability, the percentage of problems removed by these programs depends on the percentage of participating households with the problems in the first place.) Clearly, the overriding housing problem for low-income elderly renters is affordability.

Homeowner voucher participants in a voucher program are more likely to have deficiency problems and less likely to have affordability problems than rental voucher participants. Vouchers for homeowners are projected to remove structural deficiencies for almost 27 percent of participants, maintenance deficiencies for almost 8 percent, and excess cost burdens for almost 30 percent.

Unfortunately, the annual costs projected for an expanded renter or homeowner program ($3.3 billion and $5.2 billion, respectively)--given the resource constraints faced by the federal government now and in the foreseeable future--make funding for either program unlikely (and for a combined owner/rental voucher program even more unlikely).

Restricting such vouchers for the elderly also raises a potential political problem in terms of equity among generations. It would be difficult--and seemingly unfair--to distribute new allocations of vouchers to income-eligible households simply on the basis of age, even if age is correlated with certain housing-related problems. Programs more sharply targeted on the special needs of the elderly might be more acceptable to policymakers.

In this respect, a congregate housing voucher program has considerable appeal. It would be directed to the functionally impaired--who are predominantly the elderly. It would also be an "existing" housing program in the sense that congregate facilities are privately financed and developed, and are open to unsubsidized as well as voucher households. Funding responsibility for the vouchers could be divided between (HUD) and other agencies. HUD could support the housing component of the subsidy and another federal, state, or local agency (or agencies) could pick up the remainder.

APPENDICES

Appendix A

ADDING AHS VARIABLES TO THE AGED CPS FILES

This appendix describes the final predictive functions that were used to assign values to the aged CPS files.[1] Given that we were working with a fairly constrained set of explanatory variables, we were reasonably successful in estimating models which had coefficients that frequently were significant and had signs (i.e. positive or negative) in anticipated or plausible directions. Some models, of course, fared better than others. In general, the functions for predicting maintenance defects, head and spouse activity limitations, and dwelling modifications were weaker than others.[2]

Table A.1 displays the parameter estimates for the final models. The dependent variables are listed across the top of the table; the names of the independent variables appear in the left column. The total degrees of freedom is listed near the bottom of the table along with other statistical information for each model. In many cases, the degrees of freedom reported in the table do not reflect the full original AHS sample size because random samples were drawn to reduce computing costs. Table A.2 defines the variables used in the models.

A few variables in table A.2 required further explanation. First, the variables XSTRCDEF and XMAINDEF were used on the HUD/Simonson definitions of housing deficiencies.[3] Second, because predicted house values were in 1978 dollars, these amounts had to be inflated to 1984 levels using inflation factors derived from AHA and Census data.[4] Note that all statistics for the function predicting mobile home value should be interpreted cautiously, since most mobile home values were imputed using a function based on the 1983 AHS.

TABLE A.1 SUMMARY OF PARAMETER ESTIMATES FOR EQUATIONS USED TO ADD HOUSING VARIABLES TO THE CPS

	XSTORIES[a]	XROOMS (O)[b]	XROOMS (R)[c]
INTERCEPT	-0.279	-0.120	-0.331
XSTORIES			
XROOMS			
XNDEBT			
XHIEXPEN			
XSTRCDEF			
XMAINDEF			
XHLIMIT			
XSLIMIT			
XHAGE	0.002**	-0.001**	0.0002
XSAGE			
XFEMHEAD	0.021**	0.023**	0.070**
XADULTS		0.045**	0.147**
XBLACK			
XHSGRAD			
XHHY			
XELDYQ2	-0.012	-0.0005	0.049**
XELDYQ3	0.012	0.021	0.084**
XELDYQ4	0.077**	0.129**	0.176
XYNGYQ1	0.059**	0.027	0.145**
XYNGYQ2	0.043**	0.043**	0.186**
XYNGYQ3	0.032*	0.105**	0.236**
XYNGYQ4	0.057**	0.265**	0.279**
XREGNNE	0.209**	0.120**	0.114**
XREGNNC	0.039**	0.050**	0.122**
XREGNS	0.025**	0.004	0.052**
XINSMSA	0.053**	0.007	0.020**
XHEMPLOY			
XSEMPLOY			
XHTYPSF		0.251**	0.361**
XHTYPMH		0.019	0.039**
XUNITS	0.011*		
XSUBSIDY			0.074**
XINUNITS		0.001	0.040**
DEP. VAR. MEAN	0.208	0.301	0.323
TOTAL DEGREES OF FREEDOM	9571	19185	16173
R-SQUARE	0.564	0.122	0.230
ADJUSTED R^2	0.564	0.122	0.230
PROB > F	0.0001	0.0001	0.0001

	XNDEBT (O)	XHIEXPEN (O)	XHIEXPEN (R)
INTERCEPT	-0.214	0.140	0.500
XSTORIES		0.127**	0.047**
XROOMS		0.055**	0.072**
XNDEBT		-0.149**	
XHLEXPEN			
XSTRCDEF			
XMAINDEF			
XHLIMIT			
XSLIMIT			
XHAGE	0.014**	0.001**	0.002**
XSAGE			
XFEMHEAD	0.016**	0.133**	0.131**
XADULTS	-0.027**		
XBLACK	-0.084**	0.055**	-0.018**
XHSGRAD			
XHHY		h **	h **
XELDYQ2	0.028*		
XELDYQ3	0.029*		
XELDYQ4	-0.007		
XYNGYQ1	0.012		
XYNGYQ2	-0.078**		
XYNGYQ3	-0.150**		
XYNGYQ4	-0.214**		
XREGNNE	0.053**	0.035**	-0.019**
XREGNNC	0.061**	-0.010	-0.061**
XREGNS	0.058**	-0.020**	-0.067**
XINSMSA	-0.085**	0.041**	0.084**
XHEMPLOY			
XSEMPLOY			
XHTYPSF		0.129**	0.004
XHTYPMH		0.079**	0.093**
XUNITS			
XSUBSIDY			-0.228**
XINUNITS	0.121**	-0.068**	-0.101**
DEP. VAR MEAN	0.410	0.124	0.336
TOTAL DEGREES OF FREEDOM	19229	17451	16054
R-SQUARE	0.454	0.167	0.310
ADJUSTED R^2	0.454	0.167	0.310
PROB > F	0.0001	0.0001	0.0001

(continued)

TABLE A.1 (continued)

	XSTRCDEF (O)	XSTRCDEF (R)	XMAINDEF (O)
INTERCEPT	0.164	0.144	0.049
XSTORIES			
XROOMS			
XNDEBT			
XHLEXPEN			
XSTRCDEF			
XMAINDEF			
XHLIMIT			
XSLIMIT			
XHAGE	0.0001	0.001**	-0.0001
XSAGE			
XFEMHEAD	-0.001	-0.049**	0.002
XADULTS	0.012**	-0.012**	0.003**
XBLACK	0.102**	0.098**	0.039**
XHSGRAD			
XHHY			
XELDYQ2	-0.108**	-0.073**	-0.026**
XELDYQ3	-0.134**	-0.115**	-0.027**
XELDYQ4	-0.163**	-0.135**	-0.035**
XYNGYQ1	-0.094**	-0.011	-0.015**
XYNGYQ2	-0.160**	-0.088**	-0.033**
XYNGYQ3	-0.179**	-0.111**	-0.039**
XYNGYQ4	0.186**	-0.127**	-0.041**
XREGNNE	-0.017**	0.005	0.001
XREGNNC	-0.016**	-0.019**	0.001
XREGNS	0.081**	0.119**	0.004
XINSMSA	-0.042**	-0.081**	-0.009**
XHEMPLOY			
XSEMPLOY			
XHTYPSF	0.004	0.055**	-0.001
XHTYPMH	-0.046**	-0.096**	-0.008
XUNITS			
XSUBSIDY		-0.110**	
XINUNITS	0.014**	0.014**	-0.0001
DEP. VAR MEAN	0.059	0.098	0.016
TOTAL DEGREES OF FREEDOM	19121	15918	19084
R-SQUARE	0.121	0.140	0.017
ADJUSTED R^2	0.121	0.139	0.016
PROB > F	0.0001	0.0001	0.0001

	XMAINDEF (R)	XHVALUE (O)[d]	XHVALUE (O)[e]
INTERCEPT	0.005	36693.1	7117.5
XSTORIES		43683.1**	
XROOMS		19398.9**	9521.3**
XNDEBT			
XHLEXPEN			
XSTRCDEF		-7486.1**	-5220.2**
XMAINDEF		-4216.7	-635.8
XHLIMIT			
XSLIMIT			
XHAGE	g	185.3**	109.0**
XSAGE		45.6**	49.9
XFEMHEAD	0.012**	-1763.9*	813.4
XADULTS	0.014**	-710.1**	1201.2**
XBLACK	0.080**	-12088.2**	-1827.1**
XHSGRAD		8348.6**	2262.6**
XHHY			
XELDYQ2	-0.019*	1602.5	1259.0
XELDYQ3	-0.021*	3600.9**	3407.5**
XELDYQ4	-0.045**	12151.9**	5881.5**
XYNGYQ1	0.013	5931.2**	3061.2**
XYNGYQ2	-0.015	7949.2**	3904.5**
XYNGYQ3	-0.031**	10266.1**	6758.7**
XYNGYQ4	-0.036**	24679.9**	11748.7**
XREGNNE	0.037**	-18519.7**	-7042.9**
XREGNNC	0.008*	-16914.7**	-5634.0**
XREGNS	0.021**	-19600.1**	-6166.5**
XINSMSA	-0.012**	4475.1**	-2203.8**
XHEMPLOY			
XSEMPLOY			
XHTYPSF	0.022**	-5721.2**	
XHTYPMH	-0.024**		
XUNITS			
XSUBSIDY	-0.051**		
XINUNITS	0.011**		
DEP. VAR MEAN	0.050	49966.8	16296.9
TOTAL DEGREES OF FREEDOM	16083	17502	3124
R-SQUARE	0.041	0.317	0.255
ADJUSTED R^2	0.040	0.316	0.250
PROB > F	0.0001	0.0001	0.0001

(continued)

TABLE A.1 (continued)

	XHLIMIT[f]	XSLIMIT[f]	XMINMOD (O)[f]
INTERCEPT	-0.318	-0.163	0.030
XSTORIES			-0.005
XROOMS			
XNDEBT			
XHLEXPEN			-0.009
XSTRCDEF			
XMAINDEF			
XHLIMIT			0.218**
XSLIMIT			0.196**
XHAGE	0.005**		
XSAGE		0.004**	
XFEMHEAD	0.041**		
XADULTS			
XBLACK	0.009**	0.004	
XHSGRAD	-0.022**	-0.022**	
XHHY	h **	h	g
XELDYQ2			
XELDYQ3			
XELDYQ4			
XYNGYQ1			
XYNGYQ2			
XYNGYQ3			
XYNGYQ4			
XREGNNE	0.013	0.002	
XREGNNC	0.012	-0.003	
XREGNS	0.015*	-0.005	
XINSMSA	0.006	-0.006	
XHEMPLOY	-0.028**		
XSEMPLOY		-0.026**	
XHTYPSF			0.009
XHTYPMH			-0.002
XUNITS			
XSUBSIDY			
XINUNITS			
DEP. VAR MEAN	0.082	0.062	0.060
TOTAL DEGREES OF FREEDOM	11661	5331	7342
R-SQUARE	0.036	0.023	0.083
ADJUSTED R^2	0.035	0.021	0.083
PROB > F	0.0001	0.0001	0.0001

a. Sample restricted to units in structures with 3+ units.
b. Sample restricted to owners.
c. Sample restricted to renters.
d. Sample restricted to unit types other than mobile homes.
e. Sample restricted to mobile homes.

	XMINMOD (R)[f]	XMAJMOD (0)[f]	XMAJMOD (R)[f]
INTERCEPT	0.017	0.008	-0.001
XSTORIES	0.024**	0.029*	0.106**
XROOMS			
XNDEBT			
XHLEXPEN	-0.005	0.002	0.002
XSTRCDEF			
XMAINDEF			
XHLIMIT	0.143**	0.049**	0.093**
XSLIMIT	-0.035	0.048**	0.102**
XHAGE			
XSAGE			
XFEMHEAD			
XADULTS			
XBLACK			
XHSGRAD			
XHHY	g	g	g
XELDYQ2			
XELDYQ3			
XELDYQ4			
XYNGYQ1			
XYNGYQ2			
XYNGYQ3			
XYNGYQ4			
XREGNNE			
XREGNNC			
XREGNS			
XINSMSA			
XHEMPLOY			
XSEMPLOY			
XHTYPSF	0.010	0.003	0.005
XHTYPMH	0.075*	-0.011	-0.015
XUNITS			
XSUBSIDY	0.122**		0.083**
XINUNITS			
DEP. VAR MEAN	0.067	0.018	0.055
TOTAL DEGREES OF FREEDOM	2405	7342	2405
R-SQUARE	0.077	0.016	0.087
ADJUSTED R^2	0.074	0.015	0.084
PROB > F	0.0001	0.0001	0.0001

f. Sample restricted to households where age of head is 65 or over.
g. Positive value less than 0.0001.
h. Negative value greater than -0.0001.
**Significant at the 0.05 level (two-tailed significance probability).
*Significant at the 0.10 level (two-tailed significance probability).

TABLE A.2 VARIABLE DEFINITIONS

VARIABLE[a]	DEFINITION
XSTORIES	Unit has 4+ stories
XROOMS	Unit has 7+ rooms (owners); unit has 5+ rooms (renters)
XNDEBT	Own unit free and clear
XHIEXPEN	Housing expenditure as a percent of household income is greater than 30 percent
XHVALUE*	House value
XMINMOD[b]	Minor dwelling modification
XMAJMOD[c]	Major dwelling modification
XSTRCDEF	Structural defect(s) present (HUD/Simonson definition)
XMAINDEF	Maintenance defect(s) present (HUD/Simonson definition)
XHLIMIT	Head of household has activity limitation(s)
XSLIMIT	Spouse has activity limitation(s)
XHAGE*	Age of head of household
XSAGE*	Age of spouse
XFEMHEAD	Head of household is female
XADULTS*	Number of adults
XBLACK	Head of household is black
XHSGRAD	Head of household finished high school
XHHY*	Total household income
XELDYQ2	Household income quartile 2: age of head 65+
XELDYQ3	Household income quartile 3: age of head 65+
XELDYQ4	Household income quartile 4: age of head 65+
XYNGYQ1	Household income quartile 1: age of head <65
XYNGYQ2	Household income quartile 2: age of head <65
XYNGYQ3	Household income quartile 3: age of head <65
XYNGYQ4	Household income quartile 4: age of head <65
XREGNNE	Unit located in Northeast census region
XREGNNC	Unit located in North Central census region
XREGNS	Unit located in South census region
XINSMSA	Unit located inside a SMSA
XHEMPLOY	Head of household has wage salary, etc. income
XSEMPLOY	Spouse has wage, salary, etc. income
XHTYPSF	Type of unit: one-unit house/apt./flat
XHTYPMH	Type of unit: mobile home
XUNITS*	Number of units in structure
XSUBSIDY	Unit is subsidized or publicly-owned (renters only)
XINUIT5	Head of household has resided in unit 5+ years

a. All variables are dummy variables except for those marked by an asterisk (*).

b. Includes: extra handrails or grabbars; door handles instead of knobs; push bars on doors; special wall sockets or light switches; raised lettering or braille; specially equipped phone; or flashing lights.

c. Includes: ramps; elevator or stair lift; extra-wide doors; special sinks, faucets or cabinets; or bathroom designed for wheelchair use.

Because most of the variables being predicted were dichotomous, a predicted value was compared to a critical value (usually the mean value of the dependent variable), and a value of zero or one was assigned to the recipient record depending on whether the predicted value was less than or greater than the critical value. When use of the mean as a critical value yielded implausible results, the critical value was adjusted until the unweighted distribution of the imputed variable matched the unweighted distribution of that variable on the 1978 AHS file among elderly households. This procedure was necessary to produce "constant preference" files for 2010.

Missing values for two variables, XINSMSA and XUNITS, were fairly common on the aged CPS files. SMSA data were often suppressed for observations because of confidentiality requirements. Because we felt it was important to control for location in and out of metropolitan areas, we still included XINSMSA in our equations. When imputing values for the CPS files, we substituted the national mean value for this variable into the predictive functions if a value for it was missing. A value was imputed for XUNITS only if a household resided in a mobile home, in which case XUNITS was set to one. Regressions were estimated only using observations with non-missing values. Fortunately, missing values for XUNITS appear to be randomly distributed across various types of housing units, and should therefore not systematically bias our results.

Missing values were generated among appended variables when observations in the Aged CPS files contained missing values for the independent variables that appear in the predictive functions. These missing values in appended variables appeared to be randomly distributed; thus, we were able to construct a "complete" dataset by deleting observations with missing values, and proportionally increasing the weights of the remaining cases.

Although chapter 2 provided a brief overview of the methodology used to create the three sets of projections which were alternatives to the base case projections, a few additional details concerning the implementation of changed housing preferences should be noted. To simulate the situation where the elderly have the housing preferences of middle-aged households, values for the explanatory variables XHAGE and XSAGE (if applicable) were reduced by 25. This was done, however, for only four predictive variables: XSTORIES, XROOMS, XSTRCDEF, and XMAINDEF. While predicted values for these variables were directly affected by the age reduction, other variables--specifically XHIEXPEN, XHVALUE, XMINMOD, and XMAJMOD--were only affected indirectly. The variables XNDEBT, XHLIMIT, and XSLIMIT were not affected at all. The direct and indirect effects of changing the values of the age variables can be traced by examining the connection between dependent and independent variables in table A.1. For example, XHAGE is an explanatory variable for the predicted variable XSTORIES, which in turn, is an explanatory variable for the predicted variable XMINMOD.

Notes, appendix A

1. A different Aged CPS file was created and used for each of the four alternative sets of projections presented in chapter 2.

2. The parameter estimates for the functions that predict activity limitations, housing expenditures, and dwelling modifications differ from those presented in an earlier report (see Struyk, et al., 1987). We corrected the values of some variables and respecified some equations to make them more useful for our policy simulations.

3. See appendix E, table E.3 for a complete description of the HUD/Simonson indices.

4. See Struyk et al., 1987, table B.4 for details.

Appendix B

ADDITIONAL ADJUSTMENTS CONSIDERED FOR THE MAIN SIMULATIONS, AND ADDITIONAL TABLES

The following four adjustments to the simulations presented in the text were considered but ultimately rejected for the various reasons outlined.

1. Reduce the share of elderly households who are homeowners at the end of the period in light of the substantial reduction in the rate of return to homeownership that has occurred in recent years due to higher mortgage interest rates and reduced income tax advantages that have resulted from the legislated reduction in marginal tax rates. While this appears to be a reasonable adjustment, it is necessary to recall that all those who will be 65 years of age in 2010 are already 40 years old or older. Most of these households who are likely ever to become homeowners have already done so. Hence, the amount of reduction in homeownership rates for this group will be less for these households than for their younger counterparts. Still, there may be some reduction among older households (those over 75 years of age), since when they do relocate, the economic advantages of homeownership will be less. Ultimately, we decided such tenure changes were too speculative to implement, especially in light of the provisions oft he 1986 federal tax reform legislation.

2. Reduce the share of households receiving housing assistance. According to the estimates presented in chapter 2, there would be about 1.8 million elderly households receiving assistance in 2010, compared to about 0.85 million shown by the 1978 Annual Housing Survey data. While the rate of growth in the number of households receiving assistance seems very optimistic under current budget conditions, the absolute level for 2010 does not appear to be large. A recent study estimated that about 2.0 million elderly households were receiving assistance in 1985, based on program data.[1] For this reason, and because little growth in the number of households assisted by traditional housing programs is in prospect, it seems wise to leave the 2010 figure alone. In other words, the number of assisted households shown for 2010 is probably correct for the mid-1980s, and holding it constant for the balance of the period appears reasonable.

3. Adjust the incidence of activity limitations to reflect recent developments. It may be that greater life expectancy is associated with lower incidence of activity limitations at each age level. If this were the case, then the estimates presented in the last section in which age-specific activity limitations over the projection period are assumed to be constant could overstate the need or dwellings with special modifications in the future. It is also worth noting that the estimated incidence rates for 2010 are already fairly low for households headed by those 65-84 and are much higher for the oldest households. Hence, unless the changes in prospect are quite dramatic, there was a strong argument for not adjusting our estimates. In fact, a careful review of the

relevant literature shows that there is very little agreement on morbidity trends for the elderly and that the factual basis for monitoring trends in activity limitations is even weaker. On this basis, we decided not to adjust our estimates.[2]

4. Reduce the incidence of dwelling deficiencies. Several analyses of data from the American Housing Survey indicate that in the past decade there has been a modest reduction in the incidence of this type of housing problem, both in general and among the elderly.[3] At the same time, there is evidence that at least among the elderly the incidence of maintenance problems is on the increase.[4] To some extent, these trends will be captured in simulations which employ changed housing preferences, since the homes occupied by the middle-aged are generally in quite good condition. Further adjustments to these rates seemed too speculative to embody in the simulations.

Notes, appendix B

1. Struyk (1985), table 3.

2. See Manton (1980), Fries (1980), Rice and Feldman (1983), Verbrugge (1984), Palmore (1976), Palmore (1986), Manton and Soldo (1985).

3. National Association of Home Builders (1986), table 2-1; Struyk and Turner (1984), tables 3 and 4; Irby (1986).

4. Struyk and Turner, ibid.

TABLE B.1 SELECTED ATTRIBUTES OF ELDERLY-HEADED HOUSEHOLDS BY TENURE IN 1978 (percentages)

	Owner	Renters	Renters Not Paying Cash Rents
Type of unit			
house/apartment	92	96	94
mobile home	9	2	5
other	a	2	1
Units in structure			
1	90	20	79
2-4	7	30	13
5-9	1	12	4
10+	2	38	3
Unit in structure with four or more stories (1=yes)	1	22	a
Large unit occupied (1=yes)	19	19	46
Unit occupied for at least five years (1=yes)	86	53	74
Total households (millions)	11.3	4.1	.4

a. Less than .05.

TABLE B.2 DEFICIENCIES WHICH CAUSE A HOUSING UNIT TO BE JUDGED PHYSICALLY INADEQUATE - BASED UPON AHS ITEMS, REVISED DEFINITION (1981) (HUD/Simonson Definition)

Type of Deficiency	Description of Deficiency
Plumbing	1.[a] Lacks or shares some or all plumbing facilities. The unit must have hot and cold piped water, a flush toilet, and a bathtub or shower--all inside the structure and for exclusive use of the unit.
	2.[a] Lacks adequate provision for sewage disposal. The unit must be connected with a public sewer, septic tank, cesspool or chemical toilet. (Units with this deficiency are almost invariably defined as having a plumbing deficiency as well.)
Kitchen	3.[a] Lacks or shares some or all kitchen facilities. The unit must have an installed sink with piped water, a range or cookstove, and a mechanical refrigerator--all inside the structure and for exclusive use of the unit.
Physical Structural	4. Has three or more of five structural problems. Leaking roof; open cracks or holes in interior walls or ceiling; holes in the interior floors; either peeling paint or broken plaster over one square foot of an interior wall; evidence of mice or rats in last 90 days.
Common Areas	5.[a] Has three or more of four common area problems: no light fixtures (or no working light fixtures) in common hallway; loose, broken, or missing stairs; broken or missing stair railings; no elevator in building (for units two or more floors from main building entrance in buildings four or more stories high).

Table B.2 (Continued)

Type of Deficiency	Description of Deficiency
Heating	6.[a] Has unvented room heaters which burn oil or gas. If unit is heated mainly by room heaters burning gas, oil, or kerosene, the heaters must have flue or vent.
Electrical	7.[a] Lacks electricity.
	8.[a] Has three out of three signs of electrical inadequacy. One or more rooms without a working wall outlet; fuses blown or circuit breakers tripped three or more times during last 90 days; exposed wiring in the house.

a. Item included in the definition of structural deficiency; other items are included in the definition of maintenance deficiency.

Appendix C

POPULATION AND HOUSEHOLD PROJECTIONS TO 2010 USED IN TRIM2

In this appendix we describe briefly the demographic assumptions being employed in simulating the demographic characteristics of the population in the year 2010. The simulations are generated by means of a microsimulation model, called TRIM2, which is described more fully in appendix B. In very simple terms, the TRIM2 model requires as input the following items:

1. An input data file containing information on a sample of households. For this purpose, we are using the March 1985 Current Population Survey.[1]

2. Population projections by age, sex, and race for the year 2010. For this purpose, we employ projections provided by the U.S. Census Bureau and published in "Census Projections of the Population," Series P-25, Number 952, May 1984.

3. Projections of the number of households by age of head of household and type of household for the year 2010. These projections were generated by The Urban Institute, but they are based on projections of households to the year 2000 provided by the U.S. Census.

The projections that we have used, and the assumptions behind them, are described in more detail below.

POPULATION PROJECTIONS IN 2010

The population projections to the year 2010 are drawn directly from the Census publication referenced above.

Three alternative forecasts are provided; we have chosen the "middle of the road" scenario, which is entitled Series B. This series is based on population estimates by age, sex, and race as of July 1, 1982, which have been projected forward using the cohort component method and certain assumptions regarding fertility and mortality. Specifically, ultimate completed cohort fertility of 1.9 births per woman is assumed to be first attained by the 1985 birth cohort for Whites and other races, and by calendar year 2050 for Blacks. Rapid declines in mortality rates are assumed to the year 2005, decreasing more slowly thereafter, reaching an ultimate life expectancy of 81.0 years in 2080. Net immigration is assumed to be a constant inflow of 450,000 per year, which is consistent with the levels observed over the last decade.

In table series C.1, we display the population projections used as input into the TRIM2 simulations. Included are the total population projections and projections of the Armed Forces, adults and children living in institutions, and adults and children living in group quarters. The latter are not of direct interest for the current project but are required for the simulations in order to maintain consistency between the population covered in the Census projection series (which includes the total U.S. population) and the population covered in the CPS input file (which excludes the Armed Forces overseas and in barracks and persons living in institutions).

HOUSEHOLD PROJECTIONS TO 2010

The second set of projections required estimate the number of households by age of household head and by household type. Five separate types of households are distinguished: 1) husband and wife households; 2) male-headed households (no spouse present); 3) female-headed households (no spouse present); 4) households with a male as the primary

TABLE C.1 POPULATION PROJECTIONS TO 2010

CPOP2[a] 2 for 2010

Age Class	White	Nonwhite	Total
Male			
0 - 1	2,873,000	841,000	3,714,000
2 - 4	4,245,000	1,241,000	5,486,000
5 - 7	4,194,000	1,214,000	5,408,000
8 - 10	4,212,000	1,192,000	5,404,000
11 - 13	4,318,000	1,187,000	5,505,000
14 - 19	9,221,000	2,426,000	11,647,000
20 - 24	8,070,000	2,043,000	10,113,000
25 - 29	7,817,000	1,991,000	9,808,000
30 - 34	7,187,000	1,696,000	8,883,000
35 - 44	15,041,000	3,412,000	18,453,000
45 - 54	17,825,000	3,457,000	21,282,000
55 - 64	14,469,000	2,251,000	16,720,000
65 - 74	8,027,000	1,085,000	9,112,000
75+	5,832,000	665,000	6,497,000
TOTAL	113,331,000	24,701,000	138,032,000
Female			
0 - 1	2,722,000	819,000	3,541,000
2 - 4	4,024,000	1,209,000	5,233,000
5 - 7	3,978,000	1,182,000	5,160,000
8 - 10	3,994,000	1,164,000	5,158,000
11 - 13	4,098,000	1,156,000	5,254,000
14 - 19	8,764,000	2,370,000	11,134,000
20 - 24	7,711,000	2,033,000	9,744,000
25 - 29	7,527,000	2,027,000	9,554,000
30 - 34	6,969,000	1,764,000	8,733,000
35 - 44	14,724,000	3,595,000	18,319,000
45 - 54	17,871,000	3,794,000	21,665,000
55 - 64	15,300,000	2,828,000	18,128,000
65 - 74	9,608,000	1,599,000	11,207,000
75+	10,911,000	1,471,000	12,382,000
TOTAL	118,201,000	27,011,000	145,212,000

(continued)

TABLE C.1 (continued)

CPOP 2 for 2010 (continued)

Age Class	White	Nonwhite	Total
Total			
0 - 1	5,595,000	1,660,000	7,255,000
2 - 4	8,269,000	2,450,000	10,719,000
5 - 7	8,172,000	2,396,000	10,568,000
8 - 10	8,206,000	2,356,000	10,562,000
11 - 13	8,416,000	2,343,000	10,759,000
14 - 19	17,985,000	4,796,000	22,781,000
20 - 24	15,781,000	4,076,000	19,857,000
25 - 29	15,344,000	4,018,000	19,362,000
30 - 34	14,156,000	3,460,000	17,616,000
35 - 44	29,765,000	7,007,000	36,772,000
45 - 54	35,696,000	7,251,000	42,947,000
55 - 64	29,769,000	5,079,000	34,848,000
65 - 74	17,635,000	2,684,000	20,319,000
75+	16,743,000	2,136,000	18,879,000
TOTAL	231,532,000	51,712,000	283,244,000

AFPOP[b]

Age Class	Male	Female	Total
14 - 19	196,000	19,000	215,000
20 - 24	524,000	93,000	617,000
25 - 29	186,000	56,000	242,000
30 - 34	120,000	24,000	144,000
35 - 44	130,000	9,000	139,000
45 - 54	6,000	1,000	7,000
55 - 64	0	0	0
65 - 74	0	0	0
75+	0	0	0
TOTAL	1,162,000	202,000	1,364,000

AINRAT[c]

Age Class	Male	Female
14 - 19	0.01080	0.00343
20 - 24	0.01621	0.00262
25 - 29	0.01448	0.00274
30 - 34	0.01142	0.00254
35 - 44	0.00829	0.00264
45 - 54	0.00709	0.00374
55 - 64	0.00898	0.00671
65 - 74	0.01770	0.01911
75+	0.07157	0.12429

ADLINS[d] for ISIMYR = 2010

Age Class	Male	Female	Total
14 - 19	123,671	38,124	161,795
20 - 24	155,438	25,286	180,723
25 - 29	139,327	26,025	165,351
30 - 34	100,073	22,121	122,194
35 - 44	151,898	48,338	200,236
45 - 54	150,847	81,023	231,870
55 - 64	150,146	121,639	271,784
65 - 74	161,282	214,166	375,448
75+	464,990	1,538,959	2,003,949
TOTAL	1,597,671	2,115,681	3,713,352

KINRAT[e]

Age Class	Male		Female	
	White	Nonwhite	White	Nonwhite
0 - 1	0.00019	0.00047	0.00020	0.00028
2 - 4	0.00031	0.00039	0.00025	0.00028
5 - 7	0.00063	0.00091	0.00051	0.00048
8 - 10	0.00183	0.00131	0.00083	0.00105
11 - 13	0.00307	0.00543	0.00169	0.00218

(continued)

TABLE C.1 (continued)

KIDINS[f] for SIMYR = 2010

Age Class	White	Nonwhite	Total
Male			
0 - 1	546	395	941
2 - 4	1,316	484	1,800
5 - 7	2,642	1,105	3,747
8 - 10	7,708	1,562	9,269
11 - 13	13,256	6,445	19,702
TOTAL	25,468	9,991	35,459
Female			
0 - 1	544	229	774
2 - 4	1,006	339	1,345
5 - 7	2,029	567	2,596
8 - 10	3,315	1,222	4,537
11 - 13	6,926	2,520	9,446
TOTAL	13,820	4,877	18,697
Total			
0 - 1	1,090	625	1,715
2 - 4	2,322	823	3,144
5 - 7	4,671	1,672	6,343
8 - 10	11,023	2,784	13,807
11 - 13	20,182	8,965	29,147
TOTAL	39,288	14,868	54,156

AGGRAT[g]

Age Class	Male	Female
14 - 19	0.00189	0.00262
20 - 24	0.00472	0.00369
25 - 29	0.00509	0.00297
30 - 34	0.00059	0.00050
35 - 44	0.00301	0.00090
45 - 54	0.00361	0.00078
55 - 64	0.00249	0.00070
65 - 74	0.00540	0.00164
75+	0.00556	0.00663

AGQPOP[h] for ISIMYR = 2010

Age Class	Male	Female	Total
14 - 19	21352	28988	57976
20 - 24	44545	35538	71076
25 - 29	48257	28141	56282
30 - 34	5085	4343	8686
35 - 44	54786	16417	32834
45 - 54	76177	16835	33670
55 - 64	41325	12622	25244
65 - 74	48361	17995	35990
75+	33526	71857	143714
TOTAL	373414	232736	465472

KGQRAT[i]

Age Class	Male		Female	
	White	Nonwhite	White	Nonwhite
0 - 1	0.00050	0.00108	0.00045	0.00094
2 - 4	0.00035	0.00095	0.00029	0.00079
5 - 7	0.00027	0.00091	0.00026	0.00068
8 - 10	0.00064	0.00121	0.00044	0.00087
11 - 13	0.00057	0.00131	0.00033	0.00087

KGQPOP for SIMYR = 2010

Age Class	White	Nonwhite	Total
Male			
0 - 1	1,437	908	2,345
2 - 4	1,486	1,179	2,665
5 - 7	1,132	1,105	2,237
8 - 10	2,696	1,442	4,138
11 - 13	2,461	1,555	4,016
TOTAL	9,212	6,189	15,401

(continued)

TABLE C.1 (continued)

KGQPOP For SIMYR = 2010 (continued)

Age Class	White	Nonwhite	Total
Female			
0 - 1	1,225	770	1,995
2 - 4	1,167	955	2,122
5 - 7	1,034	804	1,838
8 - 10	1,757	1,013	2,770
11 - 13	1,352	1,006	2,358
TOTAL	6,536	4,547	11,083
Total			
0 - 1	2,661	1,678	4,340
2 - 4	2,653	2,134	4,787
5 - 7	2,167	1,908	4,075
8 - 10	4,453	2,455	6,908
11 - 13	3,814	2,561	6,374
TOTAL	15,747	10,736	26,484

a. CPOP2: The Census Series II projection of the U.S. population by simulation year, race, sex and age class (including institutionalized, group quarters and armed forces). Current Population Reports, Series P-25, No. 952, May 1984.
b. AFPOP: The Armed Forces members abroad and in stateside barracks as of 1984 by sex and age class. AFPOP 1984 -- Estimates of 7/1/84 AF Pop (CPR, P-25, No. 965) - March 84 CPS AF Pop.
c. AINRAT: The 1980 proportion of adults in institutions by sex and age class (1980 Census of Population).
d. ADLINS: Projected adult institutionalized population by simulation year, sex and age class.
e. KINRAT: The 1980 proportion of children in institutions by race, sex and age class (1980 Census of Population).
f. KIDINS: Projected population of children in institutions by simulation year, race, sex and age class.
g. AGQRAT: The 1985 proportion of adults in group quarters by sex and age class. Source: CPS Group Quarters Rate on 1985 CPS File.
h. AGQPOP: Projected adult group quarters population by simulation year, sex and age class.
i. KGQRAT: The 1980 proportion of children in group quarters by race, sex and age class (1980 Census of Population).

individual; and, 5) households with a female as the primary individual. The latter two are of particular interest since the elderly often live alone and are classified as "primary individuals." In the past, the Census has published projections of the number of households in this form which are consistent with their published series of population estimates. However, the published household projections have not been updated to be consistent with the newest set of population projections. We have obtained *unpublished* household projections from Census officials which are consistent, but these are only to the year 2000.

Based on the Census projections of households to the year 2000, we estimated the number of households in 2010 by extrapolating the trends that were apparent in the projections to 2000. This process was done separately by type of household. Table series C.2 (A-F) displays the unpublished Census projections to 2000 and the percentage change in the projected number of households for each year between 1996 and 2000. For comparison purposes, we have also shown the most recent estimate of the rate of growth in the number of households between 1985 and 1986.

For all five types of households the projected change reaches a stable pattern and we felt that it was reasonable to assume that this rate of change could be extrapolated to the 2000-2010 period. The overall rate of household growth is projected to be 1.1 percent per year. Husband-wife households are projected to grow less rapidly than any other type, with male-headed and male-primary-individual households growing most rapidly of all.

Once the overall "targets" for rate of household growth by household type were established, it became necessary to assume specific rates of growth within household types according to the age of the household head. Unfortunately, the trends in growth rates by age group do not appear to stabilize to the same degree as the trends in growth rates by household type. This point can also be seen in the preceeding tables. For example, for husband-wife households the overall rate of growth stabilizes at about .5 percent between 1996 and 2000. For households headed by

TABLE C.2A UNPUBLISHED CENSUS HOUSEHOLD PROJECTIONS -- SERIES B; HUSBAND-WIFE HOUSEHOLDS BY AGE OF HEAD AND YEAR (thousands of households)

	1985	1986	Percent Change
All Households	50,551	51,088	1.06
Under 25	2,066	1,942	-6.00
25 - 29	5,375	5,371	-.07
30 - 34	6,315	6,373	.92
35 - 44	11,782	12,200	3.55
45 - 54	8,569	8,642	.85
55 - 64	8,282	8,219	-.76
65 - 74	5,623	5,721	1.74
75+	2,539	2,621	3.23

	1995	1996	1997	1998	1999	2000
All Households	54,863	55,196	55,476	55,744	56,011	56,294
Under 25	1,233	1,157	1,116	1,086	1,071	1,064
25 - 29	3,885	3,812	3,695	3,573	3,413	3,251
30 - 34	6,136	5,863	5,618	5,358	5,143	5,010
35 - 44	14,721	14,894	15,019	15,065	15,058	14,947
45 - 54	11,631	12,059	12,431	12,739	13,133	13,557
55 - 64	7,760	7,853	8,013	8,312	8,564	8,805
65 - 74	6,170	6,140	6,075	6,024	5,965	5,922
75+	3,328	3,418	3,509	3,588	3,664	3,739

	Percentage Change From Previous Year				
Series B	1996	1997	1998	1999	2000
All Households	.61	.51	.48	.48	.51
Under 25	-6.16	-3.54	-2.69	-1.38	-.65
25 - 29	-1.88	-3.07	-3.30	-4.48	-4.75
30 - 34	-4.45	-4.18	-4.63	-4.01	-2.59
35 - 44	1.18	.84	.31	-.05	-.74
45 - 54	3.68	3.08	2.48	3.09	3.23
55 - 64	1.20	2.04	3.73	3.03	2.81
65 - 74	-.49	-1.06	-.84	-.98	-.72
75+	2.70	2.66	2.25	2.12	2.05

TABLE C.2B UNPUBLISHED CENSUS HOUSEHOLD PROJECTIONS -- SERIES B; FEMALE FAMILY HEADS BY AGE OF HEAD AND YEAR (thousands of households)

	1985	1986	Percent Change
All Households	10,174	10,378	2.01
Under 25	779	765	-1.80
25 - 29	1,211	1,242	2.56
30 - 34	1,409	1,447	2.70
35 - 44	2,579	2,689	4.27
45 - 54	1,598	1,628	1.88
55 - 64	1,135	1,123	-1.06
65 - 74	789	794	.63
75+	675	690	2.22

	1995	1996	1997	1998	1999	2000
All Households	11,984	12,133	12,280	12,412	12,552	12,701
Under 25	739	732	741	758	784	813
25 - 29	1,160	1,173	1,172	1,168	1,151	1,132
30 - 34	1,624	1,581	1,547	1,510	1,482	1,474
35 - 44	3,451	3,516	3,571	3,605	3,630	3,632
45 - 54	2,404	2,518	2,624	2,719	2,834	2,958
55 - 64	1,018	1,024	1,040	1,072	1,099	1,124
65 - 74	790	778	762	748	733	718
75+	798	810	822	831	840	849

	Percentage Change From Previous Year				
Series B	1996	1997	1998	1999	2000
All Households	1.24	1.21	1.07	1.13	1.19
Under 25	-.95	1.23	2.29	3.43	3.70
25 - 29	1.12	-.09	-.34	-1.46	-1.65
30 - 34	-2.65	-2.15	-2.39	-1.85	-.54
35 - 44	1.88	1.56	.95	.69	.06
45 - 54	4.74	4.21	3.62	4.23	4.38
55 - 64	.59	1.56	3.08	2.52	2.27
65 - 74	-1.52	-2.06	-1.84	-2.01	-2.05
75+	1.50	1.48	1.09	1.08	1.07

TABLE C.2C UNPUBLISHED CENSUS HOUSEHOLD PROJECTIONS -- SERIES B; MALE FAMILY HEADS BY AGE OF HEAD AND YEAR (thousands of households)

	1985	1986	Percent Change
All Households	2,232	2,299	3.00
Under 25	194	192	-1.03
25 - 29	241	250	3.73
30 - 34	292	307	5.14
35 - 44	518	550	6.18
45 - 54	381	391	2.62
55 - 64	310	309	-.32
65 - 74	175	177	1.14
75+	120	122	1.67

	1995	1996	1997	1998	1999	2000
All Households	2,940	3,010	3,077	3,143	3,211	3,282
Under 25	202	201	205	212	221	232
25 - 29	256	261	263	264	262	259
30 - 34	426	423	422	419	418	423
35 - 44	822	852	878	911	921	934
45 - 54	611	644	674	702	734	768
55 - 64	308	314	321	335	347	358
65 - 74	179	177	174	171	168	165
75+	136	138	139	140	141	141

	Percentage Change From Previous Year				
Series B	1996	1997	1998	1999	2000
All Households	2.38	2.23	2.14	2.16	2.21
Under 25	-.50	1.99	3.41	4.25	4.98
25 - 29	1.95	.77	.38	-.76	-1.15
30 - 34	-.70	-.24	-.71	-.24	1.20
35 - 44	3.65	3.05	3.76	1.10	1.41
45 - 54	5.40	4.66	4.15	4.56	4.63
55 - 64	1.95	2.23	4.36	3.58	3.17
65 - 74	-1.12	-1.69	-1.72	-1.75	-1.79
75+	1.47	.72	.72	.71	.00

TABLE C.2D UNPUBLISHED CENSUS HOUSEHOLD PROJECTIONS -- SERIES B; FEMALE PRIMARY INDIVIDUALS BY AGE AND YEAR (thousands of households)

	1985	1986	Percent Change
All Households	14,024	14,332	2.20
Under 25	971	958	-1.34
25 - 29	1,106	1,142	3.25
30 - 34	913	959	5.04
35 - 44	1,062	1,121	5.56
45 - 54	1,077	1,095	1.67
55 - 64	2,192	2,172	-.91
65 - 74	3,361	3,421	1.79
75+	3,341	3,464	3.68

	1995	1996	1997	1998	1999	2000
All Households	16,854	17,109	17,368	17,645	17,916	18,204
Under 25	962	954	970	996	1,034	1,077
25 - 29	1,136	1,156	1,163	1,168	1,159	1,148
30 - 34	1,322	1,316	1,317	1,314	1,319	1,341
35 - 44	1,610	1,661	1,709	1,747	1,782	1,806
45 - 54	1,585	1,657	1,723	1,781	1,853	1,930
55 - 64	1,983	1,997	2,030	2,094	2,148	2,198
65 - 74	3,746	3,728	3,689	3,657	3,617	3,581
75+	4,510	4,638	4,768	4,887	5,005	5,123

	Percentage Change From Previous Year				
Series B	1996	1997	1998	1999	2000
All Households	1.51	1.51	1.59	1.54	1.61
Under 25	-.83	1.68	2.68	3.82	4.16
25 - 29	1.76	.61	.43	-.77	-.95
30 - 34	-.45	.08	-.23	.38	1.67
35 - 44	3.17	2.89	2.22	2.00	1.35
45 - 54	4.54	3.98	3.37	4.04	4.16
55 - 64	.71	1.65	3.15	2.58	2.33
65 - 74	-.48	-1.05	-.87	-1.09	-1.00
75+	2.84	2.80	2.50	2.41	2.36

TABLE C.2E UNPUBLISHED CENSUS HOUSEHOLD PROJECTIONS -- SERIES B; MALE PRIMARY INDIVIDUALS BY AGE AND YEAR (thousands of households)

	1985	1986	Percent Change
All Households	10,168	10,522	3.48
Under 25	1,332	1,302	-2.25
25 - 29	1,874	1,947	3.90
30 - 34	1,404	1,472	4.84
35 - 44	1,792	1,932	7.81
45 - 54	1,004	1,042	3.78
55 - 64	1,062	1,071	.85
65 - 74	915	941	2.84
75+	785	816	3.95

	1995	1996	1997	1998	1999	2000
All Households	13,666	14,028	14,383	14,735	15,087	15,452
Under 25	1,180	1,157	1,164	1,183	1,217	1,256
25 - 29	1,989	2,028	2,042	2,050	2,033	2,011
30 - 34	1,993	1,977	1,966	1,945	1,937	1,955
35 - 44	3,312	3,478	3,636	3,779	3,912	4,020
45 - 54	1,804	1,922	2,033	2,137	2,259	2,390
55 - 64	1,165	1,197	1,239	1,303	1,361	1,417
65 - 74	1,120	1,128	1,126	1,128	1,127	1,129
75+	1,103	1,140	1,177	1,210	1,242	1,274

	Percentage Change From Previous Year				
Series B	1996	1997	1998	1999	2000
All Households	2.65	2.53	2.45	2.39	2.42
Under 25	-1.95	.61	1.63	2.87	3.20
25 - 29	1.96	.69	.39	-.83	-1.08
30 - 34	-.80	-.56	-1.07	-.41	.93
35 - 44	5.01	4.54	3.93	3.52	2.76
45 - 54	6.54	5.78	5.12	5.71	5.80
55 - 64	2.75	3.51	5.17	4.45	4.11
65 - 74	.71	-.18	.18	-.09	.18
75+	3.35	3.25	2.80	2.64	2.58

TABLE C.2F UNPUBLISHED CENSUS HOUSEHOLD PROJECTIONS -- SERIES B; PROJECTED NUMBER OF TOTAL HOUSEHOLDS BY AGE HEAD AND YEAR (thousands of households)

	1985	1986	Percent Change
All Households	8,6789	8,8620	2.11
Under 25	5,438	5,159	-5.13
25 - 29	9,637	9,953	3.28
30 - 34	10,377	10,558	1.74
35 - 44	17,481	18,491	5.78
45 - 54	12,628	12,798	1.35
55 - 64	13,073	12,893	-1.38
65 - 74	10,851	11,053	1.86
75+	7,305	7,714	5.60

	1995	1996	1997	1998	1999	2000
All Households	100,308	101,475	102,585	1,203,680	104,776	105,933
Under 25	4,316	4,201	4,198	4,234	4,327	4,442
25 - 29	8,427	8,431	8,334	8,223	8,018	7,801
30 - 34	11,500	11,161	10,870	10,545	10,297	10,203
35 - 44	23,916	24,401	24,813	25,098	25,301	25,339
45 - 54	18,035	18,801	19,486	20,078	20,812	21,603
55 - 64	12,233	12,385	12,643	13,117	13,519	13,903
65 - 74	12,006	11,952	11,826	11,728	11,610	11,516
75+	9,876	10,144	10,414	10,657	10,892	11,126

	Percentage Change From Previous Year				
Series B	1996	1997	1998	1999	2000
All Households	1.16	1.09	1.07	1.06	1.10
Under 25	-2.66	-.07	.86	2.20	2.66
25 - 29	.05	-1.15	-1.33	-2.49	-2.71
30 - 34	-2.95	-2.61	-2.99	-2.35	-.91
35 - 44	2.03	1.69	1.15	.81	.15
45 - 54	4.25	3.64	3.04	3.66	3.80
55 - 64	1.24	2.08	3.75	3.06	2.84
65 - 74	-.45	-1.05	-.83	-1.01	-.81
75+	2.71	2.66	2.33	2.21	2.15

a person under 25 years, however, the annual rate of growth varies between -6.2 percent and -.7 percent over this same period. On the other hand, the households with older heads do appear to have a relatively stable growth rate pattern between 1996 and 2000. Given that, we assumed that within household types, the growth rates by age of head would continue to follow the same pattern that was apparent in the projections between 1999 and the year 2000.

Table C.3 shows the steps involved in achieving our final household projections for the year 2010. First, projections by household type to the year 2000 are repeated in the top panel of the table. The assumed annual rates of growth for the period 2000-2010 are shown in the next panel. Given the assumed annual rates of growth by age group, households in 2010 were estimated and the percentage distribution by age of head was calculated. This distribution is shown in the third panel. Finally, we assume that the targeted growth rates by type of household are specifically achieved in 2010 and that the percentage distribution by age of head (within household types) implied in panel 3 is also achieved. This yields the final estimate of the number of households by type and age of head as shown in the bottom panel.

RECONCILING THE DEMOGRAPHIC PROJECTIONS WITH THE ACTUAL SIMULATIONS

In the two previous sections we have described the household and population projections that are required as input information into the demographic simulation routine. These essentially serve as targets that the simulation model will attempt to achieve given certain constraints. One obvious constraint is that the number of persons in projected households must be consistent with the population projection. The first step in the "aging" routine, known as POPAGE, is to calculate an "Initial Weight Multiplier" (IWM). This is a factor that, when applied to the household weight observed in the base year, results in reweighted set of households in the simulation year that achieves the household projections, or "targets", as best possible. Specifically, the IWM is calculated as the number of projected households in the simulation year (2010) divided by the number of households in the base year (1984),

$$IWM_{i,j} = CENHHB_{i,j}/HHBYR_{i,j} \; ,$$

where i = household type category, including:
1) husband/wife households,
2) female-headed households (no spouse present),
3) other male-headed households (no spouse present),
4) male primary individual households,
5) female primary individual households, and

j = age of household head, including the categories:
1) under 25 years,
2) 25-29 years,
3) 30-34 years,
4) 35-44 years,
5) 45-54 years,
6) 55-64 years,
7) 65-74 years,
8) 75 years and older.

CENHHB is defined as the Census Series B projection of U.S. households to the year 2010 (repeated in the top panel of table C.4) and HHBYR is the number of households in the input file for the base year (shown in the middle panel of table C.4).

Thus, for husband-wife households headed by a person under 25 years of age, the IWM=967000/2059023=.470. The IWM for all i and j are shown in the bottom panel of table C.4. (A and B). Obviously, the relative size of the IWM is a quick indicator of the relative growth in a particular class of household. Household categories with IWM > 1 are simulated to grow in absolute numbers by the year 2010, while those where IWM < 1 are simulated to decline in number. For example, about half as many households in

TABLE C.3 CENSUS HOUSEHOLD PROJECTIONS BY AGE OF HEAD AND HOUSEHOLD TYPE: 2000 (thousands of households)

	Husband/ Wife	Female Head	Male Head	Female Prime	Male Prime	Total	Calculated Total
All Households	56,294	12,701	3,282	18,204	15,452	105,933	105,933
Under 25	1,064	813	232	1,077	1,256	4,442	4,442
25 - 29	3,251	1,132	259	1,148	2,011	7,801	7,801
30 - 34	5,010	1,474	423	1,341	1,955	10,203	10,203
35 - 44	14,947	3,632	934	1,806	4,020	25,339	25,339
45 - 54	13,557	2,958	768	1,930	2,390	21,603	21,603
55 - 64	8,805	1,124	358	2,198	1,417	13,903	13,902
65 - 74	5,922	718	165	3,581	1,129	11,516	11,515
75+	3,739	849	141	5,123	1,274	11,126	11,126
Calculated Total	56,295	12,700	3,280	18,204	15,452	105,933	105,931
	Assumed Annual Rate of Growth 2000-2010						
All Households	.0050	.0110	.0210	.0150	.0240	.0110	
Under 25	-.0065	.0370	.0498	.0416	.0320	.0266	
25 - 29	-.0475	-.0165	-.0115	-.0095	-.0108	-.0271	
30 - 34	-.0259	-.0054	.0120	.0167	.0093	-.0091	
35 - 44	-.0074	.0006	.0141	.0135	.0276	.0015	
45 - 54	.0323	.0438	.0463	.0416	.0580	.0380	
55 - 64	.0281	.0227	.0317	.0233	.0411	.0284	
65 - 74	-.0072	-.0205	-.0179	-.0100	.0018	-.0081	
75+	.0205	.0107	.0000	.0236	.0258	.0215	

Percentage Distribution of Projected Households in 2010 by Age of Head

All Households	.501	.120	.034	.179	.166	1.000
Under 25	.016	.080	.091	.075	.086	
25 - 29	.033	.065	.056	.048	.090	
30 - 34	.063	.095	.115	.073	.107	
35 - 44	.227	.249	.260	.095	.263	
45 - 54	.305	.310	.292	.134	.209	
55 - 64	.190	.096	.118	.128	.106	
65 - 74	.090	.040	.033	.149	.057	
75+	.075	.064	.034	.298	.082	
Total	1.000	1.000	1.000	1.000	1.000	

Final Projection: Households in 2010 by Age of Head and Type

All Households	59,233	14,187	4,020	21,163	19,626	118,229	118,229
Under 25	967	1,132	367	1,580	1,684		5,730
25 - 29	1,939	928	224	1,019	1,765		5,875
30 - 34	3,739	1,352	463	1,544	2,098		9,197
35 - 44	13,464	3,537	1,045	2,015	5,164		25,224
45 - 54	18,068	4,396	1,174	2,830	4,109		30,577
55 - 64	11,272	1,363	476	2,700	2,075		17,886
65 - 74	5,343	565	134	3,162	1,124		10,329
75+	4,441	915	137	6,312	1,607		13,413
Calculated Total	59,233	14,187	4,020	21,163	19,626		118,229

TABLE C.4A U.S. HOUSEHOLD PROJECTIONS TO 2010 BASED ON CENSUS SERIES B; BY HOUSEHOLD TYPE AND AGE OF HEAD CLASS

	Husband/ Wife	Other Male	Female Head	Male PI	Female PI	Total
Under 25	967,000	367,000	1,132,000	1,684,000	1,580,000	5,730,000
25 - 29	1,939,000	224,000	928,000	1,765,000	1,019,000	5,875,000
30 - 34	3,739,000	463,000	1,352,000	2,098,000	1,544,000	9,196,000
35 - 44	13,464,000	1,045,000	3,537,000	5,164,000	2,015,000	25,225,000
45 - 54	18,068,000	1,174,000	4,396,000	4,109,000	2,830,000	30,577,000
55 - 64	11,272,000	476,000	1,363,000	2,075,000	2,700,000	17,886,000
65 - 74	5,343,000	134,000	565,000	1,124,000	3,162,000	10,328,000
75^+	4,441,000	137,000	915,000	1,607,000	6,312,000	13,412,000
TOTAL	59,233,000	4,020,000	14,188,000	19,626,000	21,162,000	118,229,000

Source: Unpublished Census Projections, projected by The Urban Institute to 2010 (3/86).

TABLE C.4B NUMBER OF HOUSEHOLDS IN THE BASE YEAR (1984) BY HOUSEHOLD TYPE AND AGE OF HEAD CLASS

	Husband/ Wife	Other Male	Female Head	Male PI	Female PI	Total
Under 25	2,059,023	195,016	784,102	1,473,373	837,424	5,348,939
25-29	5,259,032	236,360	1,199,185	1,944,112	985,826	9,624,515
30-34	6,337,380	293,458	1,410,647	1,479,604	844,782	10,365,870
35-44	11,580,347	510,536	2,545,233	1,830,045	980,675	17,446,837
45-54	8,594,358	383,371	1,599,439	1,055,976	1,030,124	12,663,269
55-64	8,363,139	313,388	1,136,517	1,122,095	2,148,723	13,083,862
65-74	5,667,744	177,227	785,680	964,460	3,307,561	10,902,672
75+	2,488,892	118,273	667,868	798,464	3,279,316	7,352,813
TOTAL	50,349,915	2,227,627	10,128,672	10,668,130	13,414,431	86,788,776

TABLE C.4C IWM: INITIAL WEIGHT MULTIPLIERS BY HOUSEHOLD TYPE AND AGE OF HEAD CLASS

Under 25	0.46964	1.88189	1.44369	1.14296	1.88674
25-29	0.36870	0.94771	0.77386	0.90787	1.03365
30-34	0.58999	1.57774	0.95843	1.41795	1.82769
35-44	1.16266	2.04687	1.38966	2.82179	2.05471
45-54	2.10231	3.06231	2.74846	3.89119	2.74724
55-64	1.34782	1.51889	1.19928	1.84922	1.25656
65-74	0.94270	0.75609	0.71912	1.16542	0.95599
75+	1.78433	1.15834	1.37003	2.01261	1.92479

Source: March 1985 Current Population Survey.

the husband-wife category headed by a person under 25 years are projected in 2010 as are reported in the input file. In contrast, over twice as many husband-wife households headed by a person 45 to 54 years are projected in 2010 as are reported in the base year.

Overall, the number of households in all categories is projected to rise from 86.8 million in the base year to 118.2 million in 2010. Each of the five household types distinguished share in this growth to some degree, but, the numbers of households is not projected to grow for all age of head classes. In general, the fastest growing class of households are those headed by a male primary individual or other male head. The number of husband-wife households are simulated to decline in the youngest age categories while other types of households are generally growing in those age categories. In the oldest age category, 75 or older, all household types are simulated to grow in absolute numbers with the greatest relative growth occurring among the female and male primary individuals.

Given the IWM, the initial reweighted number of households and the population living in households in 2010 can be calculated by household type and number of adults class. The initial number of reweighted households by household type is consistent with the projected number of households by definition. However, there is no internal mechanism to assure that the number of adults counted after reweighting is consistent with the population projection. In fact, the number of adults is a simple by-product of the reweighted set of households.[2]

One problem that arises is that the initial weight multipliers do not take into account the expected increase in the proportion of adults who live alone or in smaller household units. As a consequence, the number of adults resulting from the straightforward application of the IWM to the base year household weights will exceed the census population projects because relatively too many units with two or more adults are on the base file. To correct for this problem, a set of "scaling" factors is calculated such that the initial reweighted number of households by type will remain unchanged, but the reweighted count of adults will approach control totals as much as possible.[3] The scaling factors are defined by household type and number of adults category and are shown in table C.5. For a given sample household, the final simulation year weight is the product of the observed weight in the base year, the IWM, and the scaling factor.

Final counts of households and persons in the year 2010 are presented in table C.6 (A and B). These simulated counts do not meet the targets or projections precisely, except for the simulated number of households by household type. As discussed above, the POPAGE algorithm requires that these targets for the number of households by type be met exactly, but that the number of households by age of head and number of adults may differ in the final simulation from the targets if that is necessary to satisfy the constraints mentioned above.

In table C.7 we show the percentage difference between the simulated and projected number of households. Again, the overall targets by household type are met exactly. In general, the simulation algorithm has resulted in too many husband/wife households among the youngest and oldest age of head categories. Also, the 2010 counts show an excess of female-headed households among those headed by a female under 35. For the remaining household type groups, the simulated numbers are relatively close to the projected numbers.

An analogous table is presented to show the percentage difference between the simulated and projected number of persons by sex, race, and age. From table C.8 it is immediately clear that the simulations by race are considerably off the target population counts. This is because POPAGE does not include race as a criterion for calculating IWM or scaling factors. Hence, race as a household attribute is simply carried along in the reweighting process. The Census population projections, in contrast, do carry an implicit assumption that nonwhite mortality rates are falling in an absolute and relative sense. Hence, we would expect to see a proportionate rise in the

TABLE C.5 SCALING FACTORS BY HOUSEHOLD TYPE AND NUMBER OF ADULTS CLASS

	Husband-Wife	Other Male	Female Head	Male PI	Female PI
1		1.20731	1.28939	1.05183	1.00613
2	1.19962	1.03940	1.02753	0.85176	0.91739
3	0.86094	0.89484	0.81885	0.68974	0.83647
4	0.61787	0.77038	0.65255	0.55854	0.76270
5	0.44343	0.66324	0.52002	0.45230	0.69543
6	0.31824	0.57100	0.41441	0.36627	0.63409
7+	0.22839	0.49158	0.33025	0.29660	0.57817

number of nonwhites. POPAGE is not designed to incorporate differential aging processes by race; as a result, the 2010 simulations underpredict the number of nonwhite persons.

Overall the simulated number of persons is quite close to the projected numbers. POPAGE simulates 3.1 percent too few men and 2.4 percent too many females. However, for certain age groups the discrepancies are considerably greater. For our purposes here we are most concerned with the population counts among older persons. Among the male population, the simulated counts in 2010 show about 11 percent too many men 55 to 74 years of age. There are about 10 percent too few women in the 55 to 64 age group in 2010. It is unfortunate that the age-specific population targets are not met more closely, however, keep in mind that the targeted number of households is achieved very closely. It should not be surprising that the two sets of targets cannot be met simultaneously. In that light, neither set of targets should be regarded as anything but a rough projection.

TABLE C.6A SIMULATION YEAR HOUSEHOLDS BY HOUSEHOLD TYPE BY AGE OF HEAD CLASS

TABHH Wife	Husband/ Male	Other Head	Female
Under 25	1,142,451	360,609	1,355,677
25-29	2,280,282	227,554	1,127,562
30-34	4,330,886	489,986	1,571,889
35-44	13,251,027	1,076,963	3,450,127
45-54	15,691,259	1,136,922	3,980,738
55-64	11,417,252	459,684	1,279,558
65-74	5,976,140	133,496	539,362
75+	5,143,716	134,807	883,107
TOTAL	59,233,013	4,020,021	14,188,020

TABHH PI	Male PI	Female Total	
Under 25	1,575,627	1,535,075	5,969,439
25-29	1,706,718	1,008,264	6,350,380
30-34	2,081,090	1,538,221	10,012,071
35-44	5,154,265	2,013,300	24,945,682
45-54	4,156,783	2,835,388	27,801,090
55-64	2,126,093	2,711,983	17,994,570
65-74	1,157,404	3,176,946	10,983,347
75+	1,668,032	6,342,840	14,172,503
TOTAL	19,626,011	21,162,016	118,229,081

TABLE C.6B SIMULATION YEAR PERSONS BY SEX BY RACE BY AGE CLASS

TABPER	White	Nonwhite	Total
MALE - TOTAL	***114,583,475***	***19,166,676***	***133,750,152***
0-1	2,887,093	818,362	3,705,455
2-4	4,264,820	1,227,246	5,492,066
5-7	4,185,759	1,225,138	5,410,897
8-10	4,227,110	1,206,982	5,434,092
11-13	4,724,877	1,175,805	5,900,682
14-19	9,673,877	2,017,160	11,691,037
20-24	8,026,346	1,367,565	9,393,911
25-29	6,063,823	1,093,845	7,157,668
30-34	7,041,488	1,081,479	8,122,967
35-44	17,954,538	2,590,212	20,544,749
45-54	18,877,081	2,665,001	21,542,082
55-64	13,072,014	1,418,010	14,490,025
65-74	6,921,493	700,083	7,621,576
75+	6,663,157	579,787	7,242,943
FEMALE - TOTAL	***122,558,077***	***22,569,036***	***145,127,113***
0-1	2,769,465	789,665	3,559,130
2-4	4,029,039	1,203,805	5,232,845
5-7	3,960,922	1,172,383	5,133,305
8-10	3,960,892	1,159,930	5,120,823
11-13	4,296,650	1,159,142	5,455,791
14-19	9,339,533	2,163,018	11,502,551
20-24	8,675,795	1,969,676	10,645,472
25-29	7,075,441	1,580,615	8,656,056
30-34	9,126,074	1,719,755	10,845,829
35-44	17,649,419	3,007,804	20,657,223
45-54	17,855,701	3,083,073	20,938,774
55-64	13,638,625	1,670,745	15,309,370
65-74	9,666,987	975,830	10,642,818
75+	10,513,534	913,593	11,427,128
TOTAL	***237,141,552***	***41,735,713***	***278,877,265***
0-1	5,656,558	1,608,028	7,264,585
2-4	8,293,860	2,431,052	10,724,911
5-7	8,146,681	2,397,521	10,544,202
8-10	8,188,002	2,366,913	10,554,914
11-13	9,021,527	2,334,947	11,356,473
14-19	19,013,410	4,180,178	23,193,588
20-24	16,702,141	3,337,241	20,039,383
25-29	13,139,264	2,674,460	15,813,724
30-34	16,167,562	2,801,234	18,968,796
35-44	35,603,956	5,598,016	41,201,973
45-54	36,732,782	5,748,074	42,480,856
55-64	26,710,639	3,088,755	29,799,394
65-74	16,588,480	1,675,914	18,264,394
75+	17,176,691	1,493,380	18,670,071

TABLE C.7 SIMULATED HOUSEHOLDS COMPARED TO PROJECTED HOUSEHOLDS (percentage difference)

	Husband/ Wife	Other Male	Female Head	Male PI	Female PI	Total
Under 25	+18.1	-1.6	+19.8	-6.4	-2.8	+4.2
25 - 29	+17.6	+1.8	+21.6	-3.3	-1.1	+8.1
30 - 34	+15.8	+5.8	+16.3	-0.8	-0.3	+8.8
35 - 44	-1.6	+3.1	-2.5	-0.2	-0.0	-1.1
45 - 54	-13.2	-3.2	-9.4	+1.2	+0.2	-9.1
55 - 64	+1.3	-3.4	-6.1	+2.5	+0.4	+0.6
65 - 74	+11.8	-0.7	-4.6	+2.9	+0.5	+6.3
75+	+15.8	-1.5	-3.5	+3.8	+0.5	+5.7
TOTAL*	0.0	0.0	0.0	0.0	0.0	0.0

*These targets are met precisely.

TABLE C.8 SIMULATED POPULATION COMAPRED TO PROJECT POPULATION (percentage difference)

Person	MALE			FEMALE			TOTAL POPULATION		
Age	White	Nonwhite	Total	White	Nonwhite	Total	White	Nonwhite	Total
0 - 1	+0.5%	-2.7%	-0.2%	+1.7%	-3.5%	+0.5%	+1.1%	-3.1%	0.1%
2 - 4	+0.5	-1.1	+0.1	0.1	-0.4	0.0	0.3	-0.8	0.0
5 - 7	-0.2	+0.9	0.0	-0.4	-0.8	-0.5	-0.3	0.0	-0.2
8 - 10	+0.4	+1.3	+0.6	0.8	-0.3	-0.7	-0.2	+0.5	0.0
11 - 13	+9.4	-0.9	+7.2	+4.9	+0.3	+3.8	+7.2	-0.3	+5.5
14 - 19	+4.9	-16.9	+0.4	+6.6	-8.7	+3.3	+5.7	-12.8	+1.8
20 - 24	-0.5	-33.0	-7.1	+12.5	-3.1	+9.2	+5.8	-18.1	0.9
25 - 29	-22.4	-45.1	-27.0	-6.0	-22.0	-9.4	-14.4	-33.4	-18.3
30 - 34	-2.0	-36.3	-8.6	+31.0	-2.5	+24.2	+14.2	-19.0	+7.7
35 - 44	+19.4	-24.1	+11.3	+19.9	-16.3	+12.8	+19.6	-20.1	+12.0
45 - 54	+5.9	-22.9	+1.2	0.0	-18.7	-3.4	+2.9	-20.7	-1.1
55 - 64	-9.7	-37.0	-13.3	-10.9	-40.9	-15.6	-10.3	-39.2	-14.5
65 - 74	-13.8	-35.0	-16.3	0.6	-39.0	-5.0	-5.9	-37.6	-10.1
75+	+14.2	-12.8	+11.5	-3.6	-37.9	-7.7	+2.6	-30.0	-1.1
TOTAL	+1.1%	-22.4%	-3.1%	+3.7%	-16.4%	0.0	+2.4%	-19.3%	-1.5%

Notes, appendix C

1. Demographic characteristics are measured as of March 1985, but the income variables are asked retrospectively and cover the previous year--1984. It has become standard practice to identify the base year in TRIM2 simulations with the income year, in this case, 1984.

2. Since we are not concerned with children per se in this application, we do not discuss the adjustments to the simulations that are made specific to them.

3. Mathematically the solution to this problem requires that two constraints be satisfied simultaneously. These constraints are relatively complex functions and the final solution involves solving for the roots of a polynomial.

Appendix D

ECONOMIC PROJECTIONS AND TRANSFER PROGRAM ASSUMPTIONS USED IN TRIM2 PROJECTIONS TO 2010

ECONOMIC PROJECTIONS TO 2010

In this section we describe briefly the economic assumptions being employed in simulating the economic characteristics of the U.S. population to the year 2010. The economic characteristics are simulated in several modules of the more general microsimulation model, called TRIM2, an overview of which is provided in Appendix B. In the present application we focus exclusively on one of these models--ECONAGE--which requires as input the POPAGE projections to 2010 and a set of assumptions about changes in economic variables between the base year (1984) and 2010.[1] Recall that the output from POPAGE is simply the demographic characteristics of the population as described in appendix C.

In ECONAGE approximately 14 aggregated sources of personal income are aged forward to the simulation year using assumed growth rate targets. The targets are described in more detail below. Several of the sources of aggregate income are actually comprised of one or more detailed sources of income, as reported on the input file. A listing of the aggregated and detailed sources of income and their definitions is provided in table D.1.

The assumptions we employed to simulate sources of personal income in 2010 were generally drawn from *Data Resources U.S. Long Term Review, Winter 1985-86*.[2]

DRI prepares four long-term projection series; we rely on the "trend" outlook (TRENDLONG1285) as it is regarded as

TABLE D.1 TRIM2 INCOME VARIABLES AGGREGATE AND DETAILED SOURCES

Aggregate Source	Description and Detailed Sources
WAGES	Wage and salary income
SENF	Self-employment earnings from nonfarm sources
SEF	Self-employment earnings from farm sources
SSEC	Income from social security or railroad retirement plan ZSOCS: Social security income ZRRR: Railroad retirement income
PRENT	Income from rent and royalties
INTR	Interest income
DIVD	Dividends received, including estates or trusts ZDIVDS: Dividends ZESTAT: Income from estates or trusts
WELF	Income from public assistance ZFDSSI: SSI payments ZAFDC: Income from AFDC ZOTHPA: Income from other public assistance, including General Assistance
GPNS	Income from government pensions, including federal, state or local government pensions, and military retirement. ZMLRET: Income from military retirement ZFEDPEN: Income from federal pensions ZNFPNS: Income from state and local government pensions.
WRKC	Income from workmen's compensation
VETB	Income from veteran's benefits and pensions
UNMC	Income from unemployment compensation
PPNS	Income from private pensions
OTHR	Income from alimony, child support, and all other sources ZALIM: Alimony ZOTHC: Income from other regular contributions ZOTH: Income from any other source

the mean of all the possible paths that the economy could follow between now and the end of the century. The outstanding features of the lon-term outlook include:

- ✦ Growth will be slow relative to that experienced over the period since World War II.

- ✦ Unemployment is assumed to remain near present levels on average. This level of unemployment is relatively high as compared to levels once considered achievable.

- ✦ Inflation will run slightly over 5 percent annually, on average, which is a high level by historical standards but is well below the inflation experiences of the late 1970's and 1980's.

- ✦ The federal trade deficits will remain problematic into the future and will present real constraints on the economy.

- ✦ The cyclical swings of the 1970s and 1980s will not generally characterize the economy into the future.

Selected TRENDLONG projections are presented in table D.2. Wage and salary income is assumed to grow at an average annual rate of 7.4 percent between 1984 and 2010. Self-employment earnings grow considerably more slowly--at a 2.6 percent annual rate for farm earnings and a 5.7 percent rate for nonfarm earnings. All sources of unearned income are assumed to grow at relatively high annual rates. Rental income, with average annual growth on the order of 8.1 percent, is projected to grow at the fastest rate. Income from interest and dividends is assumed to grow at about the same pace as wage and salary income. Finally, prices, as measured by the Consumer Price Index for all urban consumers, are assumed to grow at an average annual rate of 5.2 percent, or by an overall factor of 3.866, in the 26 years between 1984 and 2010. This implies a real rate of growth in wages and salaries on the order of 2.2 percent per annum. Rental income will grow by close to 3 percent per

TABLE D.2 TRENDLONG ECONOMIC PROJECTIONS FROM DRI

Variable	1984 (Act)[a]	2000 (Est)[b] ($ Billions)	2010 (Est)[c]	Growth[d] Factor 1984-2010	Average[e] Annual Growth
Wage and Salary Disbursements	$1,804	$5,789	$12,510	6.934	7.4%
Proprietors' Income					
Farm	28	32	56	1.982	2.6
Nonfarm	126	314	558	4.419	5.7
Rental Income	63	239	515	8.168	8.1
Personal Dividend Income	78	229	517	6.623	7.3
Personal Interest Income	434	1,362	2,965	6.831	7.4
CPI-All Urban Consumers (1984=100)	100	220.2	386.6	3.866	5.5

a. *Statistical Abstract of the United States, 1986.*
b. *Data Resources U.S. Long-Term Review, Winter 1985-86.*
c. Estimated from projections to 2009 presented in *Data Resources U.S. Long-Term Review, Spring 1984*. The trends between 2000-2009 from this set of projections were assumed to also characterize the newer set of projections in b. above for the years between 2000 and 2010. The growth rate between 2008 and 2009 was extrapolated to continue through 2010.
d. Slight differences in calculations are due to rounding error.
e. Compound growth rate over the 26 year period.

annum in real terms while farm income will actually decline in real terms by about 2.6 percent per year.

The assumptions in table D.2 about growth in selected economic variables were used in constructing target growth factors for the fourteen sources of income that ECONAGE simulates. The targets are constructed at the aggregate level using a two-step process. First, base year income aggregates by source are compared to levels achieved after POPAGE--that is, after demographic aging of the base file. The aging procedure by itself will generate change in income aggregates because the change in the age distribution of the population has implications for the distribution of certain economic variables. For example, if after aging there are relatively more households in the older age categories, where the incidence of pension income is presumably higher, the aggregate amount of pension income will grow simply because there are more households of that type.

In table D.3. we present the levels of aggregate income by source in the base year and after POPAGE. The growth factor implied by the aging process is shown in the fourth column of the table. Notice that pensions and unearned sources of income, such as rents, interest, and dividends are among the sources which grow the fastest due to the aging of the file. Wages and salaries grow by only 27 percent as compared to 47 percent growth in rental income.

The target growth factors for selected income sources based on DRI projections are shown in the fifth column. Since a certain amount of growth has already occurred due to aging, we scale down the actual growth factors applied in ECONAGE in order to achieve the targets precisely. The final factors used in ECONAGE are shown in the sixth column. Certain income sources, among them social security, welfare income, government and private pensions, workmen's compensation, veteran's benefits, and other income, are assumed to grow at the same rate as the overall price index on top of any growth that has occurred in the aging process. This is done so that these income sources maintain their real value across time when measured for a given household or individual.

TABLE D.3 WEIGHTED AGGREGATE PERSONAL INCOME (millions $)

Source	Base Year 1984	After POPAGE 2010	Growth Factor 1984-2010	DRI Target Growth Factor	Factor Applied ECONAGE	After ECONAGE 2010
WAGES	$1,770,717	$2,253,553	1.273	6.934	5.447	$12,275,099
SENF	126,640	172,483	1.362	4.419	3.244	559,534
SEF	8,631	11,126	1.289	1.982	1.538	17,111
SSEC	151,477	209,454	1.383	NA	3.866	809,749
PRENT	16,475	24,224	1.470	8.168	5.556	134,587
INTR	138,664	200,274	1.444	6.831	4.731	947,496
DIVD	39,745	56,537	1.422	6.623	4.658	263,350
WELF	21,821	28,594	1.310	NA	3.866	110,545
GPNS	48,686	70,404	1.446	NA	"	272,183
WRKC	6,863	9,369	1.365	NA	"	36,221
VETB	8,392	11,570	1.379	NA	"	44,731
UNMC	12,040	14,734	1.224	NA	"	56,963
PPNS	36,763	50,849	1.383	NA	"	196,583
OTHR	30,489	39,563	1.298	NA	"	152,949

Finally in table D.4 we present aggregate levels of income by source as well as he number of persons receiving this source of income in 2010. This allows the interested reader to calculate average amounts of income by source. Keep in mind that the income sources are measured in 2010 dollars.

Simulating Unearned Income in TRIM2

Previous experience has shown that certain sources of unearned income are significantly under-reported on the CPS data files. Among the most problematic sources of income have been Food Stamps, Aid to Families with Dependent Children (AFDC), and Supplemental Security Income (SSI). There is also evidence that reported figures on Federal taxes paid are not accurate. In the current application it will be important to measure cash income among elderly households in 2010 as accurately as possible. As part of ECONAGE all sources of reported income are "aged" given income-specific assumptions about growth factors between 1984 and 2010--the assumptions were outlined above. However, aged values for AFDC and SSI have been replaced with values simulated as part of TRIM2. Food Stamp benefits have not been replaced with simulated amounts because they are not part of cash income. Federal taxes have not been simulated because we are focusing on income before taxes.

ASSUMPTIONS USED IN SIMULATING SSI

Supplemental Security Income (SSI) is targeted at low-income members of the elderly, blind, and disabled population., SSI consists of a federal component and state supplements, which may vary widely across the states. Eligibility is based on income and asset holdings--there is an asset "test" to screen individuals with too high a level of assets from receiving a benefit. The benefit paid is

TABLE D.4 INCOME BY SOURCE AFTER ECONOMIC AGING TO 2010 (counts in 10,000s; amounts in 10,000,000s)

Persons by Source of Income & Current Labor Force Status

	Employed		Unemployed	
	Recipients	Amount	Recipeints	Amount
WAGES	11,618	1,150,658	708	32,961
SENF	1,226	53,883	38	688
SEF	230	1,606	5	2
WKEARN	12,435	2,5600	730	1,039
DIVD	1,835	13,100	48	166
GPNS	221	8,675	12	481
INTR	7,928	38,658	308	1,135
OTHR	942	8,913	90	632
PPNS	181	3,441	12	323
PRENT	1,133	7,052	39	177
SSEC	489	8,829	46	673
UNMC	625	3,552	206	1,551
VETB	127	1,136	13	125
WRKC	183	1,346	19	210
ZSOCS	487	8,745	45	671
ZRRR	3	84	0	3
ZFDSSI	26	291	10	109
ZAFDC	71	605	73	832
ZOTHPA	39	169	30	184
ZDIVDS	1,781	9,117	45	110
ZESTAT	110	3,983	5	56
ZVETC	127	1,136	13	125
ZMLRET	133	5,819	5	223
ZFEDPEN	28	1,304	2	90
ZNFPNS	62	1,552	6	167
ZALIM	334	4,010	27	246
ZOTHC	95	1,228	14	107
ZOTH	560	3676	52	280

Persons by Source of Income & Current Labor Force Status (cont'd)

	N.I.L.F.		TOTAL	
	Recipients	Amount	Recipeints	Amount
WAGES	1,383	4,391	1,371	1,227,510
SENF	106	1,382	1,370	55,953
SEF	11	103	245	1,711
WKEARN	1,371	1,498	14,536	28,138
DIVD	1,041	13,069	2,924	26,335
GPNS	549	18,062	783	27,218
INTR	4,465	54,956	12,701	94,750
OTHR	437	5,749	1,469	15,295
PPNS	904	15,894	1,098	19,658
PRENT	586	6,230	1,757	13,459
SSEC	3,973	71,473	4,507	80,975
UNMC	89	593	919	5,696
VETB	245	3,212	385	4,473
WRKC	104	2,066	306	3,622
ZSOCS	3,920	69,268	4,452	78,683
ZRRR	89	2,205	92	2,292
ZFDSSI	449	4,083	485	4,483
ZAFDC	305	3,900	449	5,337
ZOTHPA	116	880	185	1,234
ZDIVDS	1,000	9,587	2,825	18,814
ZESTAT	88	3,482	203	7,521
ZVETC	245	3,212	385	4,473
ZMLRET	99	3,729	237	9,771
ZFEDPEN	179	7,618	208	9,012
ZNFPNS	290	6,715	358	8,435
ZALIM	84	1,047	445	5,303
ZOTHC	73	1,060	182	2,394
ZOTH	296	3,642	908	7,598

Families by Source of Income

	Families		Unrelated Indiv.		Total	
	Recipeints	Amount	Recipients	Amount	Recipeints	Amount
VALUEFS	344	728	676	31,188	1,021	3,916

calculated by comparing income from all sources, after specific income disregards have been subtracted, to a guaranteed income standard. Our aim in simulating SSI into the future is to maintain the same relative incidence of the most recently specified rules of the program in the simulation year--2010. For example, if the earned income disregard is $65 for an individual in 1986, and if prices grow by a factor of 3.616 between 1986 and 2010, then the earned income disregard is assumed to be $235 (65*3.616) in 2010. This approach does not necessarily mirror the most likely changes to occur to SSI program features between 1984 and 2010. In fact, some program rules, such as the asset tests, historically have not been indexed in any way. Unfortunately, we have no guidance as to likely rule changes in the years to 2010. Rather than make up arbitrary rules, we chose to maintain the relative incidence of program rules as they are last known to exist.

One of the first steps in the TRIM2 simulation of SSI is to adjust the likelihood of participation in the program. Comparison of CPS data with other program data suggests that the number of participants are underreported in the CPS. TRIM2 assumes that all individuals reporting SSI in the input file are participants in the programs. In addition, eligibility is simulated and a certain proportion of the eligible nonreporters are assigned to participate. These adjustments to the participation function are shown in table D.5

The assumptions employed in the simulation of SSI program rules in 2010 are shown in table D.6

ASSUMPTIONS USED IN AFDC SIMULATIONS TO 2010

Aid to Families with Dependent Children (AFDC) is the second program simulated in TRIM2; simulated benefits replace the aged benefits that were calculated as part of ECONAGE. AFDC is targeted toward low-income families with children, but a certain proportion of the elderly are

TABLE D.5 ADJUSTMENTS TO SSI PARTICIPATION

	Proportion of Eligible Nonreporters		Assigned Participation		
	Aged Singles	Disabled Couples	Aged Couples	Disabled Couples	Disabled Children
Federal Benefit	.253	.182	0	0	1.000
Eligible State Supp. Only	.049	.280	0	0	1.000

TABLE D.6 ASSUMPTIONS USED IN SIMULATING SSI TO 2010

	Most Recent Rule (Year)	Growth Factor Year to 2010	Rule in 2010
Monthly Earned Income Disregard	$65 (1986)	CPI-- 3.616	$235
Monthly Unrestricted Income Disregard	20 (1986)	CPI -- 3.616	72
Income Guarantee--Single	336 (1986)	CPI-- 3.616	1,215
Income Guarantee--Couple	504 (1986)	CPI -- 3.616	1,822
Value of Assets--Single	2000 (1989)	ASSETS -- 5.401	10,802
Value of Assets-- Couple	3000 (1989)	ASSETS -- 5.401	16,203
State of Supplements	Vary by State	CPI -- 3.616	Vary by State

affected as heads or members of units eligible to receive benefits. Eligibility is determined on the basis of family size, income, and asset holdings. Benefits vary considerably across the states.

The simulation of AFDC eligibility and benefits is quite complex--there are a myriad of program features to consider and, while the program is implemented in a fairly uniform fashion nationwide, specific program parameters vary considerably across states. Therefore, rather than list the specific assumptions employed, it is sufficient to note that the general aim in specifying 2010 program features was to maintain the relative incidence of program rules as they are currently described. The main features for which assumptions were made can be summarized as follows:

✦ Participation in the program is simulated using a probabilistic function based on exogenous data. The likelihood of participation is further adjusted using state-specific adjustment parameters that reflect 1982 program participation.

✦ The following program parameters were adjusted state-by-state by a factor equal to the assumed change in the CPI between 1984 and 2010 (3.866): (1) maximize monthly benefit by filing unit size; (2) monthly need standard by filing unit size; (3) monthly payment standard by filing unit size; (4) the cap on deductible expenditures for child care.

✦ The maximum value of assets by state for AFDC asset screen for eligibility was adjusted by a factor equal to the assumed average change in income from rent, interest, and dividends between 1984 and 2010 (7.207).

Notes, appendix D

1. The input file is the March 1985 CPS which covers income year 1984. It is standard practice in TRIM2 simulations to identify the base year as the income year--1984 in this case.

2. Projections are presented annually from 1985 through 2000. To extend the series to 2010 we made use of previously issued projections to 2009 *(Data Resources U.S. Long Term Review, Spring 1984)* and assumed that the relative growth rate between 2000 and 2009 in that series continued to characterize the new projection and that the growth rate between 2008 and 2009 extended to 2010.

Appendix E

ADDING 1983 AHS VARIABLES TO THE 1978 AHS FILE

Despite the general completeness of the 1978 AHS data file, it is missing some key data. Financial information on the 1978 AHS file is largely limited to single-family units on less than 10 acres with no medical offices or commercial establishments present, and mobile homes on less than 10 acres. Thus, certain types of units such as condominiums, cooperatives, large-lot units, and units with medical offices or commercial establishments present were missing information on housing expenditures (e.g., mortgage payments, utilities, etc.) and mortgage status (i.e., whether or not a unit is owned free and clear). In addition, house value was missing for all types of owner-occupied units other than one unit structures on less than 10 acres with no medical offices or commercial establishments, and condominiums. This appendix presents the final forms of the functions used to impute this missing data.

In summary, a two-step procedure was undertaken to develop the estimates of home equity holdings for homeowners. In the first, a function determining the ratio of home equity to house value (E/V) was estimated using data from the 1981 Survey of Residential Finance (SRF). This survey is part of the 1980 Census and uses the Census sampling frame. Some 62,000 non-farm, privately owned residential properties are included in the sample; and a limited amount of information on the economic and demographic position of the property owners is included in addition to data on the finances of the property.[1] Demographic and economic variables common to the CPS and the SRF were used as independent variables in the functions estimated. E/V was defined as the dependent variable in these models instead of equity in order to avoid having to update the equity values contained in the SRF from 1980. With the estimate of E/V in hand, we could proceed to the second step, which was to multiply the ratio by an estimate of house values (V) for 1984.

This step turned out to be somewhat more complicated than might be anticipated, because the 1978 AHS only contains house value information on a subset of owner-occupied properties. While this omits a small share of all homeowners, we believed it important to include the full range of owner-occupied units. Importantly, the 1983 AHS contains a greatly expanded module on residential finances which includes house value and out-of-pocket housing expenses data for almost all dwelling types and ownership configuruations. We took advantage of this information to develop functions to predict housing expenses and the value of owner-occupied units for those owner unit types for which these variables were missing on the 1978 file. This in turn permitted us ultimately to add housing expense and home equity information to all 1978 units.

The specifics of the computations are as follows. Table E.1 describes the predictive functions estimated with the 1983 AHS data. The dependent variables are listed across the top of the table; the names of the independent variables appear in the left-hand column. Table E.2 provides definitions of the variables. For each equation, the sample was limited to those types of units described above which were missing housing expenditure or house value data for 1978. For example, the sample for the fourth predictive function in table E.1 was restricted to those types of owner-occupied units for which free and clear mortgage status was not recorded in the 1978 AHS. Because the functions were estimated with 1983 data, a 1978 household record that was missing data had to have its income inflated to 1983 dollars before this amount could be substituted into one of these equations. Income was inflated based on changes in owners' median income as reported in the 1978 AHS and 1983 AHS. Different inflation factors were used for each census region.

In general, these models resemble those that were used to impute values onto the aged CPS file. However, to some extent, we took advantage of the greater number of variables which were common to both the 1978 AHS and the 1983 AHS. In addition, the similarity of the two data sets enabled us to use continuous forms of some explanatory variables. The housing deficiency variables XSTRCDEF and XMAINDEF were based on the HUD/Simonson definitions of deficiency which are reproduced here in table E.3.

Separate equations for house value were estimated for three types of units: single-family structures, multi-family structures, and mobile homes. Since the predicted values were in 1983 dollars, they were deflated to 1978 levels using ratios derived from table E.4, which shows changes in house values between 1978 and 1983.

Because the variable XNDEBT (which indicates whether or not a unit is owned free and clear) is a dichotomous variable, a predicted value for this variable was compared to the mean value of the dependent variable used to estimate the function, and a value of zero or one was assigned to the recipient record depending on whether the predicted value was less or greater than this mean.

Note, appendix E

1. For more information on the Survey of Residential Finance, see U.S. Bureau of the Census (1983).

TABLE E.1 SUMMARY OF PARAMETER ESTIMATES FOR EQUATIONS USED TO ADD 1983 AHS VARIABLES TO THE 1978 AHS

	Parameter Estimates				
Variable	House Value 1 Unit	House Value 2+Units	House Value Mobile Homes	Own Unit Free & Clear	Housing Expend. As % of Household Income
INTERCEPT	-16149.1	48406.6	-8195.8	0.026418	0.254284
ELEV		264824.0**			
XROOMS	9570.5**	4426.1**	4658.1**		0.002356
XSTRCDEF	-14775.3**	-16348.3**	-5032.5		-0.013934
XMAINDEF		-37016.0*			0.063021**
XHHY83	0.8**	0.9**	0.3**	-0.000005*	
XHAGE	529.9**	406.1**	180.0**	0.010318**	-0.000862**
XBLACK	-21540.8**	-17570.0**	-1185.7	-0.061079**	0.037732**
XFEMHEAD					0.063348**
XHSGRAD	11356.2**	5433.3	2767.9**		-0.040641**
XLRGLOT	32498.1**	71730.7**	21352.3**		
XINSMSA	25592.5**	13969.1**	397.0	-0.082141**	
XREGNNE	-43808.3**	-50444.8**	-12816.0**	-0.008598	0.027767**
XREGNNC	-29442.5**	-62127.7**	-12334.6**	-0.020151	0.025175**

Variable	Parameter Estimates				
	House Value 1 Unit	House Value 2+Units	House Value Mobile Homes	Own Unit Free & Clear	Housing Expend. As % of Household Income
XREGNS	-40273.1**	-54767.2**	-9695.9**	0.031571**	0.013068*
XCONDOWN					0.040107**
XTYPESFD					-0.007821
XTYPEMH					-0.030699**
XYRINUNI	-270.5**	-341.4**	-107.2	0.0060-3**	-0.001542**
XSHOPS	9838.5				
XDOCS	63541.9**				
XROOMADD			13395.7**		
Depen. var. mean	92989.9	71343.7	22537.3	0.518	0.199
Total degrees of freedom	3064	869	2829	7609	4355
R-square	0.169	0.312	0.249	0.293	0.075
Adj. R-square	0.165	0.301	0.245	0.292	0.072
Prob > f	0.0001	0.0001	0.0001	0.0001	0.0001

** Significant at the 0.05 level (two-tailed significance probability).
* Significant at the 0.10 level (two-tailed significance probability).

TABLE E.2 VARIABLE DEFINITIONS

VARIABLE[a]	DEFINITION
XHVALUE*	Dependent variable: house value
XNDEBT	Dependent variable: own unit free and clear
XEYRATIO*	Dependent variable: housing expenditures as a percentage of household income
XELEV	Unit is in a structure with an elevator
XROOMS*	Number of rooms
XSTRCDEF	Structural defect(s) present (HUD/Simonson defintion)
XMAINDEF	Maintenance defect(s) present (HUD/Simonson definition)
XHHY83*	1983 household income
XHAGE*	Age of head of household
XBLACK	Head of household is black
XFEMHEAD	Head of household is female
XHSGRAD	Head of household finished high school
XLRGLOT	Large-lot unit (10+ acres)
XINSMSA	Unit located inside a SMSA
XREGNNE	Unit located in Northeast census region
XREGNNC	Unit located in North Central census region
XREGNS	Unit located in South census region
XCONDOWN	Condominium type of ownership
XTYPESFD	Type of unit -- single-family detached
XTYPEMH	Type of unit -- mobile home
XYRINUNI*	Number of years head has resided in unit
XSHOPS	Commercial establishment on poperty
XDOCS	Medical facility/office on property
XROOMADD	Permanent room added (mobile homes only)

a. All variables are dummy variables except for those marked by an asterisk (*).

TABLE E.3 DEFICIENCIES WHICH CAUSE A HOUSING UNIT TO BE JUDGED PHYSICALLY INADEQUATE--BASED UPON AHS ITEMS, REVISED DEFINITION (1981) (HUD/Simonson definition)

Type of Deficiency	Description of Deficiency
Plumbing	1.* Lacks or shares some or all plumbing facilities. The unit must have hot and cold piped water, a flush toilet, and a bathtub or shower--all inside the structure and for exclusive use of the unit.
	2.* Lacks adequate provision for sewage disposal. The unit must be connected with a public sewer, septic tank, cesspool, or chemical toilet. (Units with this deficiency are almost invariably defined as having a plumbing deficiency as well.)
Kitchen	3.* Lacks or shares some or all kitchen facilities. The unit must have an installed sink with piped water, a range or cook-stove, and a mechanical refrigerator--all inside the structure and for exclusive use of the unit.
Physical Structure	4. Has three or more of five structural problems: leaking roof; open cracks or holes in interior walls or ceiling; holes in the interior floors; either peeling paint or broken plaster over one square foot of an interior wall; evidence of mice or rates in last 90 days.
Common Areas	5. Has three or more of four common area problems: no light fixtures (or no working light fixtures) in common hallway; loose, broken, or missing stairs; broken or missing stair railings; no elevator in building (for units two or more floors from main building entrance in buildings four or more stories high).

Table E.3 (Continued)

Type of Deficiency	Description of Deficiency
Heating	6.* Has unvented room heaters which burn oil or gas. If unit is heated mainly by room heaters burning gas, oil, or kerosene, the heaters must have flue or vent.
Electrical	7.* Lacks electricity.
	8.* Has three out of three signs of electrical inadequacy: one or more rooms without a working wall outlet; fuses blown or circuit breakers tripped three or more times during last 90 days; exposed wiring in house.

Source: Simonson J. (1981) *Measuring Inadequate Housing Through Use of the Annual Housing Survey*. Washington, D.C.: Office of Policy Development and Research, U.S. Department of Hosing and Urban Development, pp. 84-85.

* Items included in the definition of structural deficiency; other items are included in the definition of maintenance deficiency.

TABLE E.4 REGIONAL CHANGE IN HOUSING VALUES: 1978-1984

	Median House Value[a]			% Change New Home Value[b]	Total % Change
	1978	1983	% Change	1983-84	1978-84
Northeast					
In SMSA	44.6	65.0	45.7	10.5	61
Out	39.2	53.3	36.0		50
North Central					
In SMSA	43.1	57.6	33.6	5.0	40
Out	34.0	43.2	27.0		33
South					
In SMSA	38.6	59.6	54.4	3.5	60
Out	30.5	43.6	43.0		48
West					
In SMSA	63.7	96.4	51.3	-0.6	50
Out	42.5	59.9	40.9		40

a. Specified owner-occupied only; Annual Housing Survey data.
b. Constant quality unit; from "Price Index of New One-family Prices Sold," C27-84-Q4, Table 3. The constant quality series was used as it more accurately indicates change in all units--not just new units.